GET UNSTUCK, BE UNSTOPPABLE

VALORIE BURTON

HARVEST HOUSE PUBLISHERS
EUGENE, OREGON

P9-DEB-733

All Scripture quotations are taken from the Holy Bible, New International Version®, NIV®. Copyright © 1973, 1978, 1984, 2011 by Biblica, Inc.® Used by permission. All rights reserved worldwide.

Cover by Harvest House Publishers, Inc., Eugene, Oregom.

Valorie Burton is represented by the literary agency of Alive Communications, Inc., 7680 Goddard Street, Ste #200, Colorado Springs, CO 80920. www.alivecommunications.com.

GET UNSTUCK, BE UNSTOPPABLE
Copyright © 2014 Valorie Burton
Published by Harvest House Publishers
Eugene, Oregon 97402
www.harvesthousepublishers.com

Library of Congress Cataloging-in-Publication Data
    Burton, Valorie, 1973-
    Get unstuck, be unstoppable / Valorie Burton.
      pages cm
    ISBN 978-0-7369-5678-9 (pbk.)
    ISBN 978-0-7369-5679-6 (eBook)
    1. Life change events—Religious aspects—Christianity. 2. Adjustment (Psychology)—Religious aspects—Christianity. 3. Change (Psychology)—Religious aspects—Christianity. I. Title.
    BV4509.5.B875 2014
    248.4—dc23

                                        2014019236

All rights reserved. No part of this publication may be reproduced, stored in a retrieval system, or transmitted in any form or by any means—electronic, mechanical, digital, photocopy, recording, or any other—except for brief quotations in printed reviews, without the prior permission of the publisher.

Printed in the United States of America

      14 15 16 17 18 19 20 21 22 / BP-JH / 10 9 8 7 6 5 4 3 2 1

Contents

Introduction

As I write these words, I am picturing *you*: eyes focused on these pages, your mind hoping to read words that will finally get you unstuck and moving directly toward the sincere desires of your heart. You are smart. Hopeful. Motivated. And one more thing I know about you: The word *stuck* resonates in your spirit—*and you wish it didn't.* Some part of you, if not *every* part of you, is tired of being overwhelmed by the multitude of choices in your life, paralyzed by fears that lead you to play it safe, and dreaming big dreams that never seem to be fully realized. You are ready to move forward. Perhaps you just need a few tools to show you how. I am writing this book to help you do just that.

So just what does it mean to be stuck?

Stuck is a *pattern of counterproductive thinking or behavior* that results in your not moving toward that which you desire. It is typically a result of internalized fear, confusion, chaos, overwhelm, being lost, lack of clarity, or pessimism. By this definition, being stuck is not something that happens one time. If you stumble once, get back up, and move on, you are not stuck. That's a mistake. That's life. But if you find yourself repeatedly in similar situations, struggling with similar challenges, then *stuck* is an appropriate description. Perhaps some of these ring a bell:

- Your fear of failure, rejection, or disapproval keeps you from your dreams. Instead, you pursue other goals that feel more attainable or acceptable to others.

- Your procrastination habit creates a lot of anxiety. No matter how many times you try to stop procrastinating, you seem to always find something else to do when it comes

time to get down to business with that all-important
project.

- You can't seem to get control over your schedule, but you
  cannot figure out why. You find yourself regularly frustrated that you can't get places on time, you can't get all
  your projects completed, and you can't say no to new
  requests!

- You repeatedly find yourself in relationships that are dysfunctional and unhealthy in some way. Even when you
  meet new people, the relationship may start off fine, but
  eventually you are disappointed because the same dynamic
  eventually emerges.

- You rarely, if ever, ask for what you want. You take what
  others offer and then resent that they are not giving you
  what you want.

- You have attempted to break that bad habit—overeating,
  smoking, running up debt—but your efforts only last so
  long and eventually you fall back into your old ways. You
  wonder if there is any point in trying to change anymore.

Maybe it is the setback you are still trying to overcome or the decision you now regret that sideswiped you into a ditch. Or maybe there
isn't any one event that seems to define your stuckness. Instead, *stuck*
has become a way of life. You've gotten used to it. You may not even
think of yourself as stuck anymore. You've rationalized that this is just
how life is. But deep down, you know you are settling—and you're
really not okay with that, even when you try to convince yourself otherwise. You feel a constant uneasiness—a lack of peace—about where
things stand in your life. You are somewhat in God's will, but you want
to be perfectly in His will—and that's going to mean making some
shifts and changes. Since you have taken the step of getting this book
and reading these words, I believe you are ready to get unstuck and
become absolutely unstoppable. What that looks like, I hope to help
you define on the pages that follow.

Like you, I've been stuck many times.

I write this book to you not as someone who has always been "unstoppable," but as someone who has been stuck—many times—and somehow managed to get unstuck. I also write as a coach who has personally helped hundreds of people get unstuck in their careers, relationships, finances, and even weight loss. (You'll read some of their stories in the following pages.) Each and every time, there are principles that must be internalized and embraced. Throughout this book I will reference these principles and show you the way to navigate through them.

People who know me find it peculiar when I share my struggles with procrastination. That is because they see the end result and have no idea of the sticky, counterproductive, self-sabotaging habits I had to overcome to get there. So allow me to let you in on some of my journey—the self-sabotaging, undisciplined, frustrating but common situations I repeatedly found myself in.

I am a recovering procrastinator. I say "recovering" because I fall off the wagon—often—like when it was time to write this book. You'd think that by the time an author dives into her tenth book, she has her habits all perfectly in order. I don't. I still have to wrangle that procrastination demon who whispers repeatedly, "You can write tomorrow. That deadline is not for a while. Besides, you have more outlining, organizing, and laundry to do." If you've ever found yourself avoiding what needs to get done in favor of something—anything—else, even other stuff you've been procrastinating on that now seems easier by comparison, then I bet you can relate. I say *yes* to the voice of procrastination for a while, but then there is a pivotal moment when I have to turn in the right direction and say, "No. There is writing to be done. And I am a writer. I must write." And using the many tools I'll share with you, I do.

I felt stuck in a career that wasn't the right fit. I didn't just have a job, mind you. I owned a business. But I was doing work I wasn't all that crazy about. And I did that work pretty well, which meant people kept asking me to do more of it! I didn't want to admit I didn't want to do it. Through prayer and meditation, I finally discovered what I really wanted to do—the work I am doing right now, inspiring women to live more fulfilling lives. The problem? I couldn't figure out how to make money at it. I mean, theoretically I knew how to make money—sell books and speak for a living. Simple, right? Easier said than done. But by God's grace and a lot of tenacity, today that's exactly what I happily do for a living. My pivotal moment came one day in the shower. I dragged myself out of bed to go to the office to do work I did not feel like doing, wishing I could write and speak instead. I got into the shower, and uncontrollably, the tears came. The cry of my spirit sounded like a first grader who didn't feel like going to school that day. "But I don't feel like going to work! I don't want to."

It wasn't just my emotions, though. I could sense in my spirit that God was speaking.

"It is time to make the leap," the Holy Spirit nudged.

"But how will I make it?" I protested.

"I'll show you what to do," He assured me. "You'll be afraid. You'll also be okay." And so I turned in a new direction. I made the leap. That was 2001. The Holy Spirit was right. I was afraid, very afraid. I am also okay, better than okay.

I felt stuck financially. At one point in my life, I racked up so much credit card debt that I walked around with a heavy weight on my neck. Always in the back of my mind was the constant stress of feeling under pressure and underwater. Yet I managed to walk into department stores and plop down my credit card to dig further into a hole. I took vacations funded by mounting debt. I didn't resist the urge to upgrade to a new convertible when my paid-for four-door would have been just fine with a few repairs. I was stuck in bad habits rooted in low self-esteem. "If I just look like I'm doing well," I rationalized, "then I must be doing well."

The rationalization was a lie. One night, on my knees in prayer—a plea for God to miraculously send me a lump sum that would erase the debt I had racked up—my heart was convicted. "You need to repent," I heard in my spirit. Sure that I was doing the right thing by praying for help, I was at first shocked by the suggestion. *What do I need to repent for?* I wondered. That's when the answer came. I believe it was God's voice revealing my own blind shortcoming: "I didn't tell you to get into all of that debt. You did that. I will help you undo it, but I'm not sending you the money. You will work your way out of this one." And I did. I redirected my money. Three years of no shopping and a lot of focus, and I was debt-free.

But the biggest way I was stuck was in relationships. I didn't know what to call it at the time, but after being sideswiped into a cold, hard ditch called divorce at the age of 36, I learned—through much prayer, soul-searching, and counseling—that I was codependent.

I was vaguely familiar with the word. And it certainly wasn't one I would ever have expected to apply to me. I thought that was just a phrase for the spouses and children of alcoholics. Indeed, those who have dealt with an alcoholic or drug-addicted loved one know the routine of adjusting one's own behavior to deal with someone else's irrational, dysfunctional behavior. But the same counterproductive pattern of behavior applies in multiple situations. Codependency is behaving as though abnormal behavior is normal—acquiescing and shifting to fit the needs and wants of others, usually to the detriment of one's own wants and needs. Melody Beattie describes it this way in her book *Codependent No More*:

> They [codependents] have said yes when they meant no. They have tried to make other people see things their way. They have bent over backward to avoid hurting people's feelings and, in so doing, have hurt themselves. They have been afraid to trust their feelings. They have believed lies and then felt betrayed…They have struggled for their rights while other people said they didn't have any. They have worn sackcloth because they didn't believe they deserved silk.*

I was stuck in habits I didn't even know were a problem. I was just trying to be a good person, a good Christian, love others, and be willing to sacrifice for them. But I went about it in a way that was unhealthy and left me feeling devalued and unappreciated, sacrificing the very things I knew in my heart were God's will for me. I knew something was wrong and I knew I was tired of it. Perhaps you've been there.

---

* Melody Beattie, *Codependent No More* (Center City, MN: Hazelden, 1992), 35.

A turning point came one evening as I stood in the bathroom mirror staring at the reflection looking back at me. It was time to have a heart-to-heart conversation with that woman. It was short and to the point. I was tired of crying, tired of being disappointed, tired of success in other areas and failure in this one. I had enough faith to believe I did not have to remain stuck for the rest of my life. No. I could change. I could make a decision to change. I was the one who always said to others, "You're only stuck if you choose to be stuck." And I was no longer willing to be stuck. I said this out loud:

"You are healthy and whole, and you only engage in healthy, functional relationships."

I made a decision that day to get unstuck. I took the most important step. I faced a new direction. Prior to that day, there was a little voice inside me that insisted that because I did not learn how to have a good relationship early in life (having been a child of divorce) I was doomed to a certain lane in life. It was a lie I chose to believe. That day, I chose to reverse the lie. I decided that the first half of the statement was correct: I didn't learn the best habits early in life. But the second half of the statement was incorrect. I wasn't doomed. I could learn new relationship skills, from how to choose well to how to love well.

Soon, a verse kept appearing in my path. I knew it was for me and I meditated on it often. I believe it is for you too:

> Forget the former things;
> do not dwell on the past.
> See, I am doing a new thing!
> Now it springs up; do you not perceive it?
> I am making a way in the wilderness
> and streams in the wasteland.
> (Isaiah 43:18-19)

God wants to do a new thing in you. What has occurred in the past does not need to dictate your future. The fact that you picked up this book is an indication that you desire something new, something better than the cycles that have gotten you stuck. As we begin this journey together, you have a decision to make. It is a decision to get unstuck. It is a decision to turn in a new direction. Reject the lie that change is not possible. Choose to believe the truth: With God all things are possible.

Whether getting unstuck to write this book, getting out of a career I didn't love, getting out of debt, or finally getting and giving the love God always wanted for me, I have learned that change begins when you redirect your thoughts and your actions toward what you want—despite your track record. With God's guidance and strength, you'll build a new track record.

Whatever the case for you, this book is a tool to transform your life and rewrite the script of your life. I have four goals in these pages:

1. Make you aware of the emotions and triggers that are keeping you stuck right now.

2. Give you inspiration to conquer those emotions and triggers when they arise.

3. Help you rescript your story so it epitomizes the power of God in your life.

4. Empower you to step into the amazing life God imagined for you!

There are several components of your toolbox that will empower you to accomplish these four goals:

- *Declaration.* A large part of getting stuck is simply about the language you use—how you talk to yourself about your current circumstances and about your future. Each chapter begins with a declaration. Read it out loud. Say it with feeling. Your words hold the power of life and death, and throughout the pages of this book, you will speak an amazing life into existence.

- *Inspiration.* Getting unstuck happens in small moments of inspiration and determination. Sometimes, all we need are a few words that challenge us to shift our perspective in the moment—inspiration that propels us forward. So feel free to turn to the inspiration that speaks to what is going on with you on a given day. Each chapter is brief and ends with me coaching you to get moving. I will give you an exercise to move you forward in a tangible way. Do not skip these exercises! If you actively do them, you will experience transformation. Remember, consistency is key.

- *Prayer.* At the end of each chapter is a powerful prayer. Talking to God, declaring the greatest spiritual truths of His Word, empowers your faith and calls on the supernatural. But too often as believers, we try harder to tap into our own power than we do to invite God's power to be made manifest in our lives. I include prayers because I want to give you the opportunity to surrender any frustrations, obstacles, or overwhelm in your life to God. Invite Him in. Ask for guidance, help, miracles...and I promise you will be amazed at what happens.

Move from Unstuck to Unstoppable

The goal here is that you don't just get unstuck, but you *remain* unstuck by becoming unstoppable. "Unstoppability" (yes, I made this word up, but you know what I mean!) is resilience. Resilience doesn't mean you don't stumble or fall. It doesn't mean you don't take breaks or have a need to recuperate from failures and mistakes. It means that along your path, regardless of what happens, you do what it takes to recover, heal, rebuild, and move forward. Life is unpredictable. Often, things happen that we wish didn't. The question is, will you allow your life to completely cease when challenges or negative events happen? Will you seek God's perfect will for your life? Will you have faith in the amazing things in store for you if you believe and act in accordance with that belief?

When you become unstoppable, you epitomize the power of God in your life. God is able to use you to draw people nearer to Him because they see Him when they see your testimony. They see His strength made perfect in your weakness, and they want that type of strength. They see amazing faith, grace, and miracles unfold in your life.

Something tells them it isn't just you, but the power at work *in you*—and they begin to thirst for that same power.

As you embrace these tools as your own, you will learn to use the most powerful force you have to get unstuck from the patterns that have sabotaged your potential. That force is your mind.

Let's journey together to the heights of where God is calling you. There is something more, something bigger, something better waiting for you. It's time to get unstuck so you can live the amazing life God is calling you to.

Let's get to work!

Valorie

8 Irrefutable Rules of Getting Unstuck

When I was going through one of the most difficult challenges of my life and needed to make a life-altering choice, I came across a story that described exactly how I felt at the time—aware that I needed to move forward yet afraid of the pain that would ensue if I took action. Here's the story:

After a long and particularly grueling week of work, a farmer walked into town on a Saturday night to relax at the local tavern with dinner and a drink. Problem was, he didn't stop at one drink, or even two or three. He kept drinking until the bartender flat-out refused to sell him another round. So he gathered himself up and began to stumble back home. It was only a mile walk, but in his condition, the walk took forever. He decided to take a shortcut through his neighbor's property and garden, which was filled with rosebushes. The roses hadn't quite budded yet so the bushes were really more thorns than flowers. This was dangerous for a drunk man stumbling home. When the farmer tripped over his untied shoelaces, he landed backward in a bed of thorns. He tried to push himself up quickly, but his balance was so far gone, he just landed right back where he started. He lay there for a few minutes contemplating what to do, but the alcohol got the best of him and he dozed off to sleep.

The next morning, he awoke, startled at the sight of bushes all around him. When he tried to jump up, he felt the most excruciating, stinging pain he'd ever experienced! He attempted to gently extract himself from the thorns, but the slightest movement was so painful, he decided it wasn't worth it to move at all. Instead he lay there as still as he could in the bed of thorns—hating where he was, yet paralyzed by fear at the thought of moving.

Being stuck is kind of like that. In between realizing you need to move and being completely free lies your own bed of thorns. You can get up and move forward, but sometimes it feels more comfortable to simply stay put than bear the pain of making a change—whether it is real pain or the mental anguish of procrastination, anxiety, and self-doubt.

Getting unstuck means a series of choices. When you've been stuck for a long time, that first choice to move can feel like the most agonizing. And the subsequent ones are sometimes scary, too. All are necessary if you are to break through to the amazing life God has in store for you—the life you'll have when you squash your fears and operate in total and complete faith. But it will be worth it.

1. **You can't move forward when you're still looking backward.** Stop staring at the closed door. Let go of the past. Live fully right where you are.

2. **Meditating on the obstacle only makes it bigger.** Keep your eye on your goal rather than your problem and the problem becomes smaller.

3. **Emotions are teachers.** Pay attention to the messages your emotions send you. Stop reacting to fear and start responding.

4. **Inspiration won't chase you down.** Seek it wholeheartedly and it will always appear.

5. **You can't control which thoughts show up, but you can control which ones you entertain.** Choose your thoughts very intentionally.

6. **Your words are tools.** Your words can keep you stuck or propel you forward. Be careful what you say. Choose words that energize and strengthen you rather than victimize and weaken you.

7. **What is central in your life controls your life.** Rather than center your life on the achievement of your hopes and dreams, center your life on the One who never changes.

8. **To be unstoppable, you must master this moment.** The key to getting unstuck occurs in the heat of the moment, at the height of your fear, doubt, and hesitation, when you rally your mental, emotional, and spiritual energy to take the next step forward.

Tell Yourself the Truth

Declaration

Today, I choose to listen to the divine inner wisdom that whispers
the truth to me. I will not ignore it. I will not hide from it.
I have the courage to embrace it—regardless of the fallout—for it is
God Himself speaking to me. When I follow His wisdom,
I don't stumble. I don't get stuck. When I embrace the truth
rather than fear it, I am unstoppable.

Key Points

- When you face the truth, you are free.

- Your reality won't change until you do a reality check.

- Uncover the truth about where you are and you can begin
  to draw a map to where you desire to be.

Why is it that we ignore the truth? Or even hide from it?
You had an inkling that person wasn't who they
appeared to be, but you got involved anyway…and now
you feel stuck trying to get out of the relationship.

You knew instinctively it was not the right time to make that big
purchase, but you wanted it, so you got it. Now you're stuck with the
bill and it's causing problems.

You didn't want to take on that project. In fact, your stomach
turned when you were asked to do it, but your people-pleasing personality led you to say *yes,* and now you're stuck, resentful, and completely overwhelmed!

You knew that wasn't the right career path for you, but out of fear or insecurity or bowing to what others might think, you chose it anyway.

To be clear, I don't say any of this to beat you up. I say it so we can start this journey in a place of honesty.

The first step to getting unstuck is a simple one: Tell yourself the truth and behave based on that truth. It is easier said than done. Telling the truth and acting on it ruffles people's feathers. It may make you quite unpopular. It will make you uncomfortable at times. But nothing gets people stuck more than ignoring that still, small voice that persistently speaks if only we will listen. Consider the area(s) of your life in which you currently feel stuck and write them down here:

- *in an unorganized environment*
- *financially*
- *overwhelmed w. the quantity of things to be done — not having time to plan/organize*

Now, answer this question: If God Himself were speaking from this page, writing these words to you right now, what would He have to say to you about the area(s) in which you are stuck? Write down every nudge, inkling, and spiritual message you have sensed, no matter how small.

need a plan (detailed)
delegate

Now, based on what you sense God might be telling you:

What is it time to do?

sit down + make plans
then follow them

What is it time to say?

"there is time"

What is it time to change?

how I think — there's

   Telling yourself the truth is a simple act, but one of the most courageous. It will set you free and on a path to a life that is absolutely unstoppable. So as we start on this journey, I believe God is asking you first to be truthful. Answer some simple but bold questions:

- What are you afraid to admit?
- What are you really afraid will happen if you take action?
- Whose approval are you so afraid of not gaining that you forego your dreams, your vision, and your freedom?
- What do you avoid for fear of facing the consequences of change?
- And what would you have to let go of in order to move toward the life God imagined for you?

I realize these aren't easy questions, but I believe the answers lie within you. They are so powerful that when you answer them truthfully, your next steps begin to unfold in a big way. You can run from them or ignore them, but they are not going away. That's the power of having the courage to tell the truth.

Truth awakens you from the deep slumber of lies. In pretending we don't hear the voice of the Holy Spirit or resisting the guidance of that voice, we live a lie. "God, did You say this man I'm dating is not 'the one'? But we've been together too long. I've invested too much. If I don't stay with him, then what? I'll be alone again. I'll never meet anyone else. God, that can't be You. No, that wasn't You. I'm going to stick with what I have." And more years progress and the relationship doesn't. You feel stuck.

Or maybe it's not the relationship. Maybe it's your money habits. You know God has nudged you to be a better steward, speak up, and negotiate what your contributions are worth, but the idea of doing so scares the dickens out of you. You imagine yourself groveling for a better salary and being thrown out of your boss's office, or telling the dealership you want a better price and having them laugh in your face. "No!" they might yell in disgust. "Who does she think she is?" And so you are quiet. You don't just want a better deal or higher pay, you *need* it. But feelings of insecurity may lead you to pretend all is well financially. But it is not.

If you embraced the truth of what you know deep down, you'd be free to walk onto the path God has for you—a life in which you are perfectly within His will. It is a life of faith. You step out with no guarantees except God's promise that He will never leave you nor forsake you and His declaration that if you delight yourself in Him, He will give you the desires of your heart.

Get Moving!

1. **Go to a quiet place**. For two full minutes, close your eyes and breathe deeply—slow, cleansing breaths. Breathe in

slowly for five seconds. Hold for five seconds. Then exhale for eight seconds.

2. **Meditate** on the words of Jesus found in John 8:31-32: "If you hold to my teaching, you are really my disciples. Then you will know the truth, and the truth will set you free." The truth of God's Word will always set you free, and so will the truth of your situation.

3. **Tell the truth**. After meditating on the scripture, do a reality check on your biggest challenge and answer these questions: What truth(s) have you avoided admitting to yourself? In what way(s) has this affected your ability to move forward?

Prayer

Lord, give me the courage to face the truth and not ignore it. Give me the faith to trust Your nudges when the truth makes me afraid. Empower me with boldness and courage to take actions that matter. My power lies in Your presence within me. I want to honor that presence by acting on Your guidance in all things, especially when fear tries to paralyze me. Thank You, God, for speaking to me. Now help me act based upon what I hear. Amen.

Build Your Bank of Evidence

Declaration

Today, I choose to open my eyes to the amazing miracles that have already occurred in my life—opportunities I couldn't have made happen by myself, blessings I did not expect that showed up at the perfect hour, and people who crossed my path at the right time. When I notice what God has already done, it strengthens my faith for what He can do now.

Key Points

- Like a skilled and persuasive lawyer, build a case for God's amazing track record in your life.

- Stop pointing to the reasons why you can't move forward and start highlighting the reasons why you can.

- Research shows optimists are more likely to bounce back from setbacks and succeed in the face of challenging odds.

- Noticing what went well in the past gives you confidence for your future.

Doubt is inevitable. It is one of the main ways the enemy kills, steals, and destroys dreams. If you're going to live the amazing life God always imagined for you, you've got to be equipped with an arsenal of faith. And one of the quickest ways to operate in faith is to constantly remind yourself of God's track record.

Let's do it right now. When you look back over your life, what are the three greatest ways God brought you through a challenge or set you up for victory? Consider your family life. Health. Relationships. Finances. Work. I'm sure there are more than three examples, but I'm asking you to list the three that stand out most to you:

1. _____

_____

_____

2. _____

_____

_____

3. _____

_____

_____

If God did those things, what else could He do in your life? What do you need to trust Him to do?

_____

_____

_____

_____

_____

Build a bank of evidence about God's faithfulness in your life. In the moments and even seasons when you doubt, go to your "faith bank" as a reminder of...

• just how good God has been in your life.

- His amazing and often inexplicable power to orchestrate good on your behalf.

- how many times you've doubted and yet God has come through anyway.

- the fact that all things work together for good for those who love God and are called according to His purpose (Romans 8:28).

- what happens when you trust Him.

When you build your faith bank, do so strategically. Don't just think about the areas in which you most need to build your faith. More importantly, consider the areas where you already have strong faith. Reflecting upon powerful examples in your life can build your confidence that God can do the same thing in a new area of your life.

For example, Denise has been very successful in her professional life. Colleagues jokingly refer to her as the "golden child." From the moment she graduated from school, she worked for a top company in a great job. She was promoted early and often. By the age of 30, she was already a vice president. By 32, she'd branched out and started her own company. She had great friends, plenty of money, and was in good health. There was just one thing she wanted that never seemed to work out for her: a great relationship.

Over the years, her relationships disintegrated for a number of reasons. Sometimes the men seemed insecure about her professional and financial successes. Other times, Denise simply seemed to choose guys who were simply not a match—untrustworthy, hiding serious issues, or not interested in a long-term commitment. She went to counseling. She tried downplaying her accomplishments at work. She joined dating sites. She prayed. But truth be told, she didn't believe anymore. She'd assumed this part of her life would all come together in her early twenties. Now, she felt stuck.

She started to give up on her dreams of marriage and family. "I'm blessed in so many ways. I have good friends and family, a great work life. Maybe it is too much to expect more," she said to me one day.

"There just aren't that many eligible men in my age group. They are either married or have issues or aren't interested in being with a woman who has too many professional successes."

"Really?" I asked. "You think God can do all that He's done in your life, but He can't orchestrate the right mate for you?"

"Well, He hasn't," she said.

"Yet," I said. "Let me ask you something. What is the likelihood of a college student landing the job you landed out of college?"

She perked up and smiled gratefully. "Well, there were a lot of applicants. Working for a major television network is something so many people want to do. So the competition is pretty fierce. For the program I got into, there are about ten slots and 6,000 applicants."

"Wow," I said. I knew her career had started on a high note, but I didn't realize just how amazing the odds were! "And how about all the promotions and opportunities you got in your twenties? What is the likelihood of getting promoted to VP at 29?"

She smiled again. "Now, that was incredible," she admitted. "That was totally a God thing. I had so much favor, I can't even explain it!"

"You've got favor all right," I concurred. "And your business—you know, most businesses don't last a year. Even fewer last five years."

"True," she agreed. "What's making you bring all of this up?"

"Well, it seems to me you have walked on faith in your career. You've believed big things could happen. And they have. God has blessed you against major odds. When 5,990 people didn't get an opportunity and ten did, you were one of the ten. When 90 percent of businesses that started when yours did failed, yours succeeded. The odds of your connecting with the right mate at the right time are much higher than these other desires of your heart. Maybe God is waiting on you to trust Him and really believe."

The Bible says that when we come to Him in prayer, we must ask believing He will do it. One way to boost your belief is to build your faith bank in your area of success and realize that God can do as much, if not more, in your area of need. Often, it is your faith that is being tested. When you have success in one area, it is tempting to believe you have control. Often, what you really have is favor. And what God can do in one area, He can do in another.

Get Moving!

In what area of your life do you have full confidence in the possibility of success?

_____

_____

_____

In what area of your life do you most feel stuck, as though the desires of your heart will not come to pass?

_____

_____

_____

In what way(s) did your faith get you unstuck and make you unstoppable in the area where you have been most successful?

_____

_____

_____

What did you learn from your faith in your success area that God now wants you to apply in the area where you are stuck?

_____

_____

_____

Prayer

Lord, I want more faith. I know that without faith, it is impossible to please You. Help me with my unbelief. Help me to see the power You have unleashed numerous times in my life! Today, I will set out to build a bank of evidence for Your track record in my life. I will use my bank of evidence as the foundation to believe for more than I could ever ask, think, or imagine! Help me believe in that power to free me and propel me forward. With You, all things are possible. I believe it—and today, I will act like I believe it! Amen.

Rewrite the Script

Declaration

Today, I choose to tell my story in an empowering way. If the script I've been following is not working, I can rework it. My next chapters are yet unwritten and the choices I make will fill in the pages of my life story.

Key Points

- You have the power to change your story—both the story you tell to describe the past and the one you write that will speak your future into existence.
- Pay attention to the villains and victims you've created in your script.

Ann and her sister, Janet, grew up in the same dysfunctional household. When their parents divorced when they were barely in elementary school, what was already dysfunctional became worse. No one ever seemed to put a lot of effort into raising the girls. Their mother had a steady string of boyfriends. Some were abusive to their mother, others were abusive to them. No one had particularly high standards for either of them. And they lived up to them. By the time each of them was 20, they each had two children by two fathers, had no career to speak of, and were overweight. Their relationships were constantly filled with turmoil and drama.

Ann was better off than Janet, though. The years of neglect and abuse had taken a heavier toll on Janet, and she was headed down a dark path. Ann often found herself looking for her sister, as she would disappear for days at a time without telling anyone in their family where she was. Ann knew her sister was strung out on drugs, checked out of life completely.

Ann had a job at the mall and a part-time job as a cashier at a local service station. It was hard to explain how she did it. She worked non-stop and when she wasn't working, she was taking care of her children and the household. There had always been a resilience about her. Even as children, Ann was the one to look after her sister, even though Janet was a year older. Ann seemed to find a way to keep her head up even when there was so much cause for keeping her head down. Still, she was very unhappy with the way life had turned out.

One afternoon, her boyfriend stopped by to tell her he didn't want to continue their relationship anymore. It was the last straw for Ann. It wasn't that he was such a great catch, but the fact that she'd invested so much and put up with so much from him. He had cheated. Ann forgave him. His work history was sketchy. Ann made excuses each time he'd quit irresponsibly or been fired. She had clung to the only semblance of love she'd been able to find.

But despite everything she'd been through, she had a persistent feeling that God was real and He had a plan for her life that was much better than what she'd experienced thus far. With very little education or professional skills, a family she felt betrayed by, and two children to take care of, that day brought a pivotal moment for Ann. It was the day before she had planned to sign a new lease on the small apartment she shared with her children. "There is absolutely nothing here for me," she thought. "Nothing and no one in this town will ever lead me to a better life." She dreamed desperately of love and opportunity and a better life for her kids.

She made a drastic decision. Within two weeks, Ann packed up everything she owned, asked a girlfriend to help her put her furnishings and belongings into a U-Haul, buckled her kids into the front seat beside her, and drove herself to a new life two hours away in nearby Houston. With $600 saved up, she negotiated her way into a small apartment, enrolled herself in a community college, and soon started working.

Ann rewrote the script of her life. It looked like it was going in one direction, but she hit the brakes, turned the car around, and chose a brand-new direction for her life. Not only did she go on to earn a bachelor's degree, but she finished grad school too. Others didn't expect much of her, but she made the decision to expect more of herself and to step into the kind of life God imagined for His precious daughter.

We all have the ability to do that. Whether the change you need to make is small (quit eating snack cakes from the vending machine at 3:30 every afternoon) or huge (completely start your career over), you can begin a new story line for your life starting today.

Consider your work, relationships, health, finances, and spiritual life. Which story line is it time to rewrite?

_____

_____

_____

_____

_____

What is the new story line you want to create?

_____

_____

_____

_____

_____

Consider Ann's bold move. It was courageous and definitive. Is there a bold move you feel God calling you to make? What is it?

_____

_____

_____

_____

_____

Rewrite the Story You Tell

God rewrote the script for many people in the Bible. Time after time, He changed a person's name at a dramatic turning point in their life story. Abram became Abraham. Jacob became Israel. Simon became Peter. Saul became Paul. Their names corresponded with the change in their story. Each became unstoppable to fulfill the purpose for which he was created.

What if, instead of embracing their new story, they chose to continue describing themselves by what they used to be? What kind of testimony would that have produced? Paul would have continually reminded us he was really Saul, the persecutor of Christians. But what would have been the purpose? Those labels no longer described him.

The same is true for you. What story are you telling about the pivotal moments in your life?

Sometimes where we get stuck does not necessarily involve rewriting our current script, but rewriting the story we tell about our lives. If the story you tell leaves you as the victim—powerless, bitter, or helpless—then it's time to change how you tell your story. What you say about your life and your circumstances is even more powerful than what others say.

"He left me devastated. It's been downhill ever since."

"I never got the chance to go to college and it ruined my chance for a successful career."

"I'm no good with money. It just slips through my fingers."

These types of statements keep us stuck. How do you tell the story of your challenges? What definitive statements do you make that label you in terms you don't actually want to describe you? What you say to yourself about yourself can either propel you forward or hold you back—and keep you looking back.

Reframe any aspects of your story that leave you feeling disempowered in such a way that glorifies God and grows you. Here's how:

- Describe past challenges as events you have overcome, survived, or thrived in spite of.

- Refuse to make anyone who hurt you the centerpiece of your story. They do not get a starring role in your story. Give God the starring role. Describe the ways in which God grew you, enlightened you, protected you, or helped you through the situation.

- Own any mistakes or failures you had.

- Own any good decisions you made and successes you had.

- Tie your story to the present moment in a way that celebrates your resilience and "unstoppability."

Consider for a moment an event, challenge, or situation from your past that you believe has held you back in some way. If you were to tell the story using the five points above as a guideline, how would you tell that story differently?

_____

_____

_____

_____

_____

Get Moving!

Rewrite your script. What does your life look like when you are "unstoppable"? Write a vivid description that inspires and energizes you.

_____

_____

_____

_____

_____

_____

Prayer

Lord, it is time to rewrite the script on some aspects of my life. I believe You want me to have a new story line and to stop allowing the same issues to trip me up over and over again. I want to rewrite my story in a way that glorifies You and grows me into the person You created me to be. I know that person is unstoppable—not stuck. So God, help me see Your vision for my life—the amazing life I believe You imagine for me.

Choose Your Cast and Crew

Declaration

Today, I choose carefully who I spend time with. Relationships empower me to move forward or remain stuck. Whatever courage I need to speak up, make changes, or show up differently in my relationships, I will muster that courage. My most important aim is to please God, not people. And I am at peace with the fact that sometimes it will be impossible to do both.

Key Points

- The secret to a great life is having great relationships.
- When you rewrite your script, be discerning about who plays the key roles in your life and who you play a key role for.

If you're going rewrite your script, you need a cast and crew. These are the players who make your story possible. The movie of your life would not be very interesting if you were the only starring character in it. As you rewrite your script, create a picture that is amazing—exactly as God imagined it for you. No need to play small—this is your life! The best stories are rich with characters. You need a cast and crew that does all these things:

- **Brings out your best.** To be unstoppable, you need people around you who inspire your best self to emerge. These are people who stretch and challenge you, but also love and believe in you. Being around them doesn't drain your energy. Instead, they are energizing.

- **Sparks good chemistry.** I'm not just talking about romantic sparks here (although having a member of the cast and crew who does that is a definite plus!). I'm talking about people who share your values. They get you and you get them. You are moving in the same direction. You are spiritually compatible.

- **Raises the bar.** Any actress will tell you that her breakout role was one that enabled her to test the limits of her abilities. Often that happens when one is acting alongside talented counterparts. The same is true in your own life. Include people in your cast and crew who raise the bar, inspire you, and whom you respect and admire for how they live their life. These include friends, family members, mentors, coworkers, and spiritual leaders.

- **Are better off with you.** While you play a starring role in your script, it is not all about you! In the best story, your life will have a positive effect on the people around you. You will make a difference. You have a contribution to make that serves your cast and crew, makes them better, grows them, and in some cases even inspires them to rewrite their own script! Some in your cast and crew won't have much to give, but you'll have the opportunity to learn and grow alongside them.

Not Everyone Can Play a Role

As you make your list, you may notice some people you wish you could place on one of the lists, but being honest with yourself, you cannot. Or perhaps you were even tempted to try to make someone fit your list who simply does not belong there. You're not alone. But here's one way to keep from getting stuck in a dead-end relationship: Stop expecting people to get unstuck if they don't want to. Accept them right where they are, but refuse to be stuck with them. If you have been holding your breath for someone to do right, show up, or be there for you and they simply haven't, waiting longer is probably not going to make any difference.

Stop holding your breath. Instead, exhale. Expecting something another will not or cannot give keeps you stuck in a holding pattern, waiting for them to change before you change. And without your realizing it, they become your excuse for not getting on with your life and the divine assignment it is time for you to tackle.

Make this decision: "I do not expect from someone what they will not or cannot give me." Now, with this decision, you can ask a question that will free you to move on with the business of life: "Assuming this person is not going to make a shift in their behavior, what shift do I need to make?" It is freeing to stop waiting on something that is not coming. It is empowering to realize God has a plan for your life, even if it often involves navigating around challenges and issues.

Sherry was holding out hope her boyfriend would finally decide to settle down, that he would see what a great catch she was and want to marry her. He was nice, but he was quite comfortable dating indefinitely. Sherry had committed to him, wasn't dating anyone else, and was becoming increasingly anxious and insecure about the relationship, which was neither empowering for her nor attractive to him.

"Why have you committed yourself to someone who doesn't share your vision?" I asked.

"What do you mean?" she shot back.

"You want marriage and family. He seems ambivalent about it. But you've committed to a relationship on the hopes that he will change. He's perfectly happy. You're not," I pointed out.

When you rewrite the script, make sure your cast and crew want to be in the movie you're writing. Otherwise, the story that gets written won't be the one God has placed in your heart. It will be what others decide for you. If you're not living your vision, you're probably living someone else's.

Be discerning and courageous about who plays a role in your life. Not everyone has earned the right to be in your inner circle. In fact, allowing the wrong people in can create potholes and detours on your path that take a long time to overcome. Not everyone will appreciate your spiritual maturity and faith. If you allow such an important part of who you are to be devalued by someone else, you will begin to devalue it, too.

Get Moving!

As you consider the criteria for your support system, who is officially in your cast and crew? Make a list. Becoming unstoppable requires being intentional about the people in your life. Write the names of your cast and crew in each of the below categories:

Brings out your best personally and professionally.	
Sparks good chemistry. Shares your faith and values and is easy to be with.	
Raises the bar. Stretches and challenges you as a role model or mentor and has won your respect.	
Better off with you. People you serve and help even when they can't return the favor.	

Prayer

Lord, thank You for opening my eyes to the need to be as discerning as possible about the people in my life. Help me attract the type of people whose values and interests align with my own—people who bring out my best as I bring out theirs. Give me the courage to cut off friendships that are not fruitful and the wisdom to repair relationships that are broken, but divinely orchestrated. As I rewrite the script of my life, make clear the cast and crew who are meant to play a role! Who are my confidants? Who has my back? Who should I let go and who should I embrace? To live the amazing life You've always imagined for me, I know I need the right people in my life—iron sharpeners, people who bring out my best, not my worst. And I need to nurture my relationships with those closest to me. Strengthen my relationship skills so that I am my authentic self. Help me forgive. Help me step into the shoes of others and give me greater compassion, wisdom, and understanding. Show me habits that hold my relationships back and help me transform those habits. Bless my relationships. Amen.

See Through the FOG

Declaration

Today, I choose to seek clarity about why I am stuck. I don't get stuck by accident. I get stuck for specific reasons. Once I understand those reasons, I can intentionally avoid them. By gaining knowledge about the causes, I can tap into the wisdom that will set me free from the patterns that tend to trip me up. It is a choice to open my eyes and see beyond the fog.

Key Points

- The reasons you get stuck fall into three categories. These three categories spell out the acronym FOG.

- Choose self-awareness by identifying what has you stuck and making a decision to move beyond it.

One morning, I turned out of my neighborhood to head to my office and was startled by what appeared to be a cloud of smoke across a wide swath of gray sky. The tall buildings that normally tower over the nearby streets were nowhere to be seen. It was a bit disorienting.

As I tried to make sense of it, I had only one thought: *There must be a fire.* I scanned the area while driving, curious what building the fire might be coming from. But as I continued to drive down the street, I realized the "smoke" expanded far beyond the few blocks from home. It wasn't smoke at all. It was a dense fog—thicker than I've ever seen in my life! I continued on to work and traffic was slow, even for my then two-mile commute. Amazingly, an hour later when I stepped out of my office, the sun's bright rays had parted the fog and the skyline was in clear view. Finally, there was clarity.

It reminded me of what happens when life gets foggy and cluttered. It can feel like you can't see the next step, what decisions to make, or whether what has always been there is still there at all. It is like wading through a dense fog of uncertainty and confusion.

Should I follow my dream or play it safe? Should I buy the house now or keep renting? Should I go back to school so I can change careers or stay in this career I don't enjoy? Should I hold on to this relationship or let go? While working with clients over the last decade and even in my own life, I have noticed that stress and stagnancy are often created by a lack of clarity. It is normal to feel uncertain and fearful of the future when you can't see clearly.

Once you get clear, it is like rays of sun burning away the fog of confusion—and suddenly you are no longer stuck.

Typically, you get stuck for one of three reasons (which happen to form the acronym FOG):

- **F**ear
- **O**verwhelm
- **G**od's will and your will don't match

It can be argued that fear is the foundation for the other two categories, but each of these is distinct and different. Think about the areas in which you feel stuck. This issue that paralyzes you likely fits into one of these three categories.

Fear

You are afraid of what will happen if you move forward. Whether you fear rejection or failure or success or other people's opinions, fear is a powerful paralyzer. Get clear about the fear and conquer it, and nothing will be able to stop you. Not sure if fear is your issue? Here are some ways to know:

- You don't ask for others' help because you don't want to hear *no*.

- You don't ask for feedback because you are afraid of what criticism you might receive.

- You don't speak up because you don't want to offend anyone.

- You're afraid to do too well because people will expect you to keep it up, and that feels like way too much pressure.

- The idea of failing feels like the worst thing in the world. Failing makes you feel like a failure, and you'll avoid that label at all costs.

- You just don't know if you're good enough to accomplish what you really want to accomplish. If you step out in faith and can't do it, you'll just prove you're not good enough. Better to stay safe than to prove your inadequacy for all the world to see.

- Because of insecurities, you overcompensate by overspending, overeating, or being a pushover, for example. You constantly make decisions that are nothing more than emotional reactions to deep-rooted fears.

Overwhelm

Especially in today's world, with so many options, expectations, and "to-do's" waiting to be checked off your never-ending to-do list, it is easy to feel overwhelmed. The sheer volume of stuff vying for your attention can crush you. Picture yourself trying to hold it all up until finally the weight of everything overtakes you and you are flattened like a pancake in a Bugs Bunny cartoon. That's how it feels sometimes. Your job is to be intentional about setting boundaries around your life. These boundaries protect you from being overwhelmed, thereby keeping you from getting stuck under the weight of expectations. Not sure if overwhelm has you stuck? Here are some of the signs:

- You are gifted and have so many options of what to do with your life that you are afraid to choose any out of fear you might make the wrong choice! For example, you have the talent to go in multiple career directions. There are many suitable mates who'd love the chance to be with you. With so many options, you feel no sense of urgency. In fact, you may take your choices for granted or have trouble seeing clearly the purposeful path God has for you.

- You don't like to say *no*. In fact, you hate the idea of disappointing people or having them think you are selfish or unconcerned about the needs of others. So you say *yes* to everything. Then you stress out trying to do it all, and you may even feel resentful about "always having so much to do" or "never having time for you."

- The project that needs to get done feels so big you don't even know where to get started—so you simply don't start. You analyze it, talk about it, and even strategize. But for some reason, you don't actually do it.

God's Will and Your Will Don't Match

The third way we get stuck is simply by insisting upon doing things our way. This can occur for any number of reasons—you decided God was taking too long so you moved forward on your own, you didn't like the direction God was leading you so you chose a different direction, or you are just not spiritually in tune with your life. Here are a few ways that we get stuck as a result of being out of God's will:

- You ignored that still, small voice that tried to direct you, and now you find yourself in a situation you are struggling to undo.

- Your relationship with God is waning and you really haven't even thought to pray and ask for His will in the situation in which you are stuck. It perhaps hasn't even occurred to you that you're stuck because you are in the wrong place. Maybe the doors aren't opening because God doesn't want them to.

- God's will isn't just about where you are ultimately meant to be, but also about the timing of when you should be there. Sometimes, you feel stuck because the timing is off. Whether the right moment has passed or it hasn't yet come, seek God's will for timing. Once you let go of the notion that your timing is the right timing, you are free.

See beyond the FOG. Which of the three categories explain why you feel stuck right now? Take a moment now to get clear.

Area in which you are stuck	Primary Reason
	☐ Fear ☐ Overwhelm ☐ God's will/your will don't match
	☐ Fear ☐ Overwhelm ☐ God's will/your will don't match
	☐ Fear ☐ Overwhelm ☐ God's will/your will don't match

Get Moving!

Coach yourself with a few questions to clear the fog and begin to see your way through.

What is unclear to me right now?

_____

_____

_____

What specific information or activity will give me clarity?

_____

_____

_____

Who or what resources do I need in order to get that clarity?

_____

_____

_____

What decision will clarity empower me to make?

_____

_____

_____

Why is that decision important for me right now?

_____

_____

_____

Prayer

Lord, when I try to see my way clear, sometimes I just feel as though I cannot. Help me get crystal clear about what has me stuck. I know You are not the author of confusion. Help me see what You see so I can go where You want me to go. Whatever lesson I need to learn, Lord, make it clear to me. And with the knowledge of the lessons, give me the wisdom to navigate the obstacles that appear on my path. Your Word promises that if I lack wisdom, all I have to do is ask and You'll give it to me. I am asking now, God. I am listening expectantly. Thank You in advance that the answer You want me to see is about to appear. Amen.

Get Specific, Really Specific

Declaration

Today, I choose to take specific steps toward my goal. I won't just dream big; I'll determine the concrete actions that will help me achieve that dream. I choose to stop making excuses that prevent me from moving forward.

Key Points

- In order to get to your goal, you need to be specific about what you want to achieve. The more specific your goal, the more obvious your next action becomes.

- Start big and vague and then narrow it down.

We always hear how important it is to tap into your strengths, but what about when your strengths actually hold you back and get you stuck? It happens to me all the time. One of my favorite strengths assessments, the Value-Impact Assessment, describes my signature strength as "hope, optimism, and future-mindedness." That strength is confirmed with Gallup's Strengthsfinder, where one of my top five strengths is described as "futuristic." I get super excited about the future and the possibilities. That's great when I'm coming up with goals, dealing with a setback, or running my company. But when I'm stuck and need to get really specific about the next step, it can be a problem. As a visionary, I can see the big picture clearly. And I can get you to see it, too—and taste it and feel it and even smell it. But ask me what the very next step is to move in that direction, and the answer doesn't always come so naturally. Can you relate?

Through research, psychologists have developed what they call "goal setting theory." In it, they describe a set of approaches that must be present in order to be highly effective in both setting your goals and getting to your goals. One of the approaches is simply described as "Specificity." In other words, to effectively get to your goal, you need to be super specific about the goal. The more specific your goal, the more obvious and specific your next action steps become. Vague goals lead to vague steps—and can even cause you to feel paralyzed. It is the feeling of knowing where you need to go, grabbing the keys to hop in the car, and then wondering, "Hmm. Too bad I don't have a navigation system because I don't have a clue which direction to go first." You can be completely riled up about what's next without actually knowing the obvious: what to do next. So you sit at the driver's wheel, ready to go, but spin your wheels.

Specificity is a powerful tool. Let's try using it right now. Think about what has you stuck today. Maybe you've been sitting in front of the computer with a message or project that needs to be written. Perhaps you have been contemplating a conversation without a clue how to start it up. Perhaps you want to redesign a space in the house, but don't know where to begin. Maybe you are overwhelmed about the prospect of losing weight and don't believe you can manage all the steps people are telling you to take and wonder which step would have the most impact. You know where you're stuck. Write it down right here:

_____

_____

_____

_____

Get Moving!

Now, rather than starting with "What step do I need to take next?" begin with the goal. You can start big and vague and then narrow it down. I'll guide you with some questions that will help you do just that.

What's the goal?

_____

_____

_____

What will reaching this goal empower you to do?

_____

_____

_____

By which date do you want to accomplish the goal?

_____

_____

_____

What will it give you to accomplish this goal?

_____

_____

_____

Quantify that goal. Depending on the details of the goal, there is a good chance you can quantify it with numbers (total amount, dollars, pounds, number of people, size of the space, etc.—the relevant number will depend on what the goal is). What measurable number can you apply to the goal?

_____

_____

_____

Be as specific as possible. If you were in your perfect world, what are the specific details of how this goal would come together?

_____

_____

_____

_____

_____

Prayer

Lord, if You are not the author of confusion then You must be the author of clarity! And I need clarity right now, Father. Your Word tells us that where there is no vision, the people perish. I've seen that happen in my own life. I've been lost without a vision—stuck, not because I am unwilling to move, but because I do not know where to move. Help me remember that knowing specifically where You want me empowers me to know what steps to take to get there. I am reading these pages right now because I believe it is Your will for me to be unstoppable—to bounce back again and again for Your glory. I don't just want a vision. I want Your vision for me. What is it, God? Show me in vivid detail. Paint a picture of what You've always imagined for me so that my imagination can see it and run with it. Yes, run! Your vision for me will give me the energy, the passion, and the strength to move from a stuck place to an unstoppable place. It is a vague vision that has left me in a foggy place. The power of pinpointing a specific goal for which to aim will be like a sunrise that clears away the fog, revealing the majestic landscape that was always there. Lord, I want to see the majesty of the amazing life You imagine for me. Open my eyes! Amen.

Adjust Your Normal

Declaration

Today, I want my life to look different—to exemplify divine purpose over pop culture. I choose to live at a pace that reflects God's wisdom more than cultural norms. Just because everyone else lives an overloaded, overdriven lifestyle doesn't mean I have to.

Key Points

• You might not recognize how overwhelmed you are because your life is no different from the ones around you. It's time to take a step back and reevaluate what *normal* looks like.

• If you're stressed out and stretched beyond your capacity, you won't be able to step into the amazing life God has for you.

O f the three culprits of being stuck represented in FOG (fear, overwhelm, and God's will versus your will), overwhelm is the culprit that has probably been most affected by changes in our culture in recent decades. In fact, many people who are overwhelmed either don't recognize the problem or don't believe they *should* be overwhelmed. There are a couple of common reasons for this lack of awareness.

First, in many circles overwhelm is the state everyone lives in. The expectation is that you *should* be doing ten things at once. After all, isn't everyone else doing just as much or more? It is possible you don't recognize how overwhelmed you are because you are no different from everyone around you—at work, at home, or in your community at large. In essence, overwhelm is your norm. So I invite you to stop for a moment and ask yourself, "Is this the normal I want? Is this the normal God intended for me?"

I believe Jesus would refuse to live the kind of lives most of us live. Throughout Scripture, as Jesus's journey is described, He is never described as doing too much. In fact, we are surprised to see how often He retreats from the crowds for time with His Father and closest followers.

The question you must ask yourself as a believer is whether you want to live the way God created you to live or whether you want to live stretched beyond capacity, stressed, and so overwhelmed that you feel paralyzed. It may take some radical thinking and drastic action steps, but you have the power to choose to live differently. You have the power to choose a lifestyle that empowers you to be at *your* best without the pressure to be the best at everything. You can choose to do less and want less.

I'm not saying it won't be uncomfortable, but I'm saying that it is a choice. That fact ought to encourage you. You have choices—even more choices than you may currently realize. You can adjust your normal to a state that is more palatable and manageable for you. It may require lifestyle changes or it might simply be a matter of a conversation or small change you need to make. You will likely be going against the grain of what those around you are doing, but I guarantee that at least a few in your circle will either be jealous or inspired. They don't like being overwhelmed either, and your decision to live differently will challenge their own choices.

The second reason for the lack of awareness about the culprit of overwhelm is this: You may be too hard on yourself. You might actually believe that despite everything on your plate, you should not be overwhelmed. In other words, you think something must be wrong with you. If you were just more organized or more disciplined or more efficient, all would be well. You actually believe that the CEO mom who manages to have a family does it all by herself. You actually imagine that the woman at work who appears to have it all together never gets in an argument with her husband and her kids are perfect and she's got the world all figured out. And because you believe that, you are hard on yourself when you struggle to get unstuck from the challenges and cycles that persist in your life.

If this is your thought process, I invite you to let it go. You are normal if overwhelm has set in. In fact, this is God's way of communicating with you since your life is too noisy for His still, small voice to even be heard. Overwhelm is a warning. It is the Holy Spirit's signal to you that you need to do something different. Otherwise, don't you think you'd have the grace and anointing to remain on the track you are on?

So here's my challenge to you. Adjust your normal. When you feel overwhelmed, it is a signal to move counter to the cultural, community, or business norms that are not the way God created you to operate. Here's how to make an adjustment:

1. Recognize overwhelm as a warning signal.

2. Prayerfully seek God's norm for you in this season of your life.

3. Take action to allow your schedule and obligations to reflect your chosen normal.

When we are overwhelmed, we make mistakes as we rush through our days, trying to get as much done as possible. Worse than that, often what we accomplish is not actually what is most important or effective. It takes thought to be effective—not the kind of thinking that occurs when we multitask, but the kind of thinking that requires reflection, intention, and being in tune with God. With so many other thoughts, distractions, and to-do's fogging up the vision, it is pretty difficult to hear your own thoughts, let alone hear from God.

What happens when you are overwhelmed?

1. You have a short fuse.

2. You are rude or curt with others. Other people are just an interruption, adding to your stress.

3. The fog of activity and pressure makes it hard to clearly

discern what to do next, thereby leaving you unable to see your way forward.

4. The overloaded lifestyle makes activities, opportunities, and relationships that should bring you joy nothing more than another item on your already long list of to-do's.

5. Goal fatigue sets in as you deplete the energy needed to reach multiple goals—even the simple ones. As a result, you find you do not have the stamina or discipline to stick with your plans.

Get Moving!

Adjust your normal. Coach yourself with these questions:

What events and occurrences have recently been a warning about the state of overwhelm in your life? (Perhaps you find yourself constantly late, arguing with your spouse, being resentful of scheduled obligations, or missing deadlines at work.)

_____

_____

_____

Get in a quiet place. Pray. And listen for that still, small voice that is nudging your spirit. What is God's norm for you in terms of the state of your schedule? How does that norm match up with your current reality?

_____

_____

_____

Take action. What changes do you need to make in order to adjust your normal to a state that leaves you feeling energized and purposeful, even if it looks different from those around you? List every change, conversation, or adjustment that needs to take place.

_____

_____

_____

_____

_____

_____

_____

Prayer

Lord, I realize that in some ways my life is out of alignment for what You intended. The pace and sheer volume of obligations is more than I can handle. Even if the obligations cannot be changed in this season, show me the adjustments You need me to make in order to be in Your perfect will. Help me live at a pace that empowers me to actually enjoy all the blessings in my life rather than feeling burdened by them. Give me the grace to do what You are calling me to do. Open my eyes to the warning signals You need me to see. I want my normal to reflect Your wisdom, not the "wisdom" of the world. Amen.

Do It. Delay It. Delete It.

Declaration

Today, I choose my obligations intentionally. I obligate myself only to that which God asks of me. When I become overwhelmed, I remember that I create my schedule. I have the power to prune my activities so they align with my current season of life and the divine assignments to which I am called.

Key Points

- Overwhelm causes you to get stuck by paralyzing you. You cannot move forward on anything because you feel pulled in multiple directions and don't know which one to begin first.

- Activating your power to prioritize, postpone, and prune is the key to moving your schedule from overwhelming to manageable.

One of the things I've loved about being a coach is that I seem to attract a lot of friends who also coach, and sometimes our conversations turn into "coaching conversations." That's professional speak for, "I'm no longer just chatting with you. I'm asking non-judgmental, self-reflective questions and giving you the space to answer without injecting my personal opinion." I'm being a little tongue-in-cheek, but it is true. A while back, I was feeling overwhelmed. (Overwhelm is the FOG that most often gets me stuck.) I was really looking forward to brunch with my friend Yvette after church that Sunday because I was hoping our chat would take a turn toward a coaching conversation. I needed that nudge to help me break out of the heavy, overloaded schedule that was stressing me out. That's exactly what happened.

As I described the ridiculously full but purposeful schedule I had coming up, we arrived at some solid conclusions about new actions I should take to keep the cycle from repeating itself. The most significant thing she said was, "Take a look at everything on your calendar and put it in one of three categories. Do it, delay it, or delete it."

Do it.

Items in the "do it" category are diverse. There are some things on your calendar you need to get done. You are already committed. There is no undoing it. If you could press the rewind button on your life, maybe you would decline these opportunities, but you can't press rewind. You suck it up and do it. It is a matter of simply digging your heels in and getting it done.

Other things on your calendar may be priorities you absolutely *want* to do. Now, when you're feeling overwhelmed, *everything* on your to-do list stresses you out, but these things are nonetheless right in the center of your purpose. Make a decision about when you will do them. Actually consider how long they will take, when the best time will be, and what resources or people you need in order to complete the task. Set a date. Make calls, if needed. Put it on the calendar. Do it!

Delay it.

I don't know about you, but I've certainly been known to stress myself out with self-imposed deadlines or to agree to deadlines my gut told me were too tight. Truth is, much of what stresses us out is actually negotiable. Although we feel the world will come crashing in if we don't get it "all" done by a certain date, it won't. When you look at everything on your plate, look with a truth lens at which deadlines are "hard deadlines" and which ones are not.

For example, if you're pregnant, the baby is coming. The baby might be late by a couple of weeks, but not by a couple of months! A close friend of mine was scheduled to have a C-section to deliver twins on a certain day. Some complications arose and she went to the hospital. To her total shock, they told her they were going to take the babies that day. It was three weeks earlier than "scheduled." As they wheeled the bed to the operating room, she began explaining to the nurses, "No, they aren't supposed to come yet! I have three more weeks." To which the nurse replied, "Umm, no you don't."

That's a hard deadline. It's one over which you have no control or that has serious consequences beyond your control if you miss it. If you've ever gotten a ticket for forgetting to renew your vehicle registration or paid a late fee for missing the due date on a bill, you know exactly what I mean.

Then there are the self-imposed deadlines. This includes your self-imposed deadlines for when you are supposed to reach certain milestones in your life. These are the dates or times by which you want something to happen. If it doesn't happen, you'll be annoyed or maybe even angry, but there are no consequences outside of those you inflict upon yourself. Whether it is a goal date for finishing a project or getting a promotion or the date by which you think you should be married or have a family, consider that maybe your deadline isn't on God's timeline for you.

Pray about it. If it is a project, for example, set a new and more doable deadline that will leave you feeling empowered and able to accomplish your goal well and with breathing room. If it is a life goal beyond your control, do what is within your control to put yourself in position to be ready when the dream unfolds, but be open to allowing God's timing to prevail.

If overwhelm is the FOG that keeps you from being unstoppable, loosen those self-imposed deadlines so you can breathe more easily. The stress you're under is unnecessary. Let go. You'll get unstuck.

Delete it.

Lastly, let's face it. Somehow, a lot of stuff ends up on the calendar that simply doesn't need to be there. Either it never should have made it onto the radar or you are in a new season and it no longer belongs there. One of the most powerful actions you can take is to press *delete* on these activities and obligations. Don't be afraid to do it. This is where your courage comes into play. You may have to disappoint someone as you remove yourself from a project that is no longer purposeful for you. You may be concerned that others don't see you as "nice" when you say *no* to their requests. But when you say *yes* to things God didn't call you to, you often end up saying *no* to what God *is* calling you to because you don't have the time or bandwidth to pursue it wholeheartedly.

Press delete. Say *yes* to the direction to which God is calling you. You'll literally feel your path open up. What once felt *stuck* will suddenly feel like momentum.

"If we must constantly hurry to get everything done, then we are doing too much," said a recent tweet from Joyce Meyer. If you are struggling to cram too much into your schedule, embrace the fact that there is a divine message in your overwhelm. If you were meant to do so much, don't you think God would give you the grace to do it? This explains why one person may be able to do what appears to be an extraordinary amount of activity. If you are graced to do something, it might look ridiculous to others but you won't be overwhelmed by it.

Overwhelm is a sign your capacity has been reached. Pay attention. If you go too long in this state, the consequences can be even bigger than just missing your opportunity. Your health and mental wellness could be at stake as a result of the stress. Your relationships can suffer as you attempt to juggle more than you are able and begin dropping the ball on your real priorities—people. Please pay attention. Overwhelm is a wakeup call—a gift. Respond by creating a more reasonable schedule and pace.

It isn't enough to do the "do it, delay it, delete it" routine just once. It will work once. Then you will likely start doing the same thing again—putting too much on the calendar. I've added this little routine every couple of months in order to ensure that my schedule does not run out of control and out of balance. It is actually in a reminder on my calendar. If you find yourself in a pattern of repeatedly committing to too much, schedule "do it, delay it, delete it" as often as you need to in order to keep your schedule from overwhelming you.

Get Moving!

Do it, delay it, and delete it—right now! Take a ten-minute break and pull out your schedule and to-do list. For each obligation on your list, make a decision to do it, delay it, or delete it.

Prayer

Lord, I seem to get into a cycle of overwhelming myself with too many obligations. Then I get paralyzed and can't get anything done. Help me get clear about what I need to do now, what I need to delay, and what I need to delete. I want to be in Your perfect will, and I know that will be difficult as long as I'm saying yes to what doesn't matter and no to what does. Give me the wisdom, decisiveness, and freedom to get unstuck from over-obligating myself! Amen.

Dive Below the Surface

Declaration

Today, I choose to look below the surface of my behavior to better understand what drives it. When I seek to be aware of why I do what I do, I am empowered to effectively change my behavior for the better. Anytime my actions are not consistent with what I want for my life, I choose to look below the surface and ask, "How are my beliefs about myself and my situation hindering me?"

Key Points

- Iceberg Beliefs, as they are called by psychologists, are deeply held thoughts and core values that explain your actions—or lack thereof.
- When your Iceberg Beliefs collide, you get stuck!
- Icebergs are not necessarily bad, although sometimes they are. The key is learning to navigate them.

Amanda finally saw all of her dreams on the verge of becoming true. In the past two years she'd gotten married, become guardian to her eight-year-old niece, and now she and her husband were expecting. She loved mothering her niece and was really excited about having a biological child as well. Even more, a big break was on the horizon in her career—an opportunity she had dreamed of and worked toward for more than ten years! Her boss called her into his office to tell her the news. It would mean a major pay raise and allow her to make a lasting, positive impact using her gifts and background.

She couldn't have asked for more. All she would need to do, her boss explained, was solidify the deal with a presentation to the board. This wouldn't be too difficult because she had already done the research and pitched the original idea to her boss and his peers—to obvious success! She'd need to deliver the presentation in three days, so she decided to get a head start later that evening.

But while she normally breezed through such projects, she seemed to be at a loss. And if she told herself the truth, she felt a knot in the pit of her stomach. She chose to ignore it, but she still didn't get much done that evening. As she lay in bed that night, at the end of one of the best days of her career, she didn't feel nearly as excited as she should for the magnitude of the opportunity before her. What on earth was going on?

Amanda's reaction didn't match up with the seemingly positive event that just happened. When your response is incongruent to a stressor, challenge, or opportunity, it is possible you've bumped into an iceberg.

You have deeply held beliefs—core values—that shape your thoughts and actions. These beliefs become your personal rules for how you believe the world should work and what you believe or assume to be true about yourself and others. Often, these beliefs are so ingrained that you are not even conscious of how strongly they influence your behavior. When these beliefs collide, decisions that seem like they should be easy will become inexplicably difficult. Getting clear about your iceberg requires that you ask questions that dig beneath the surface. Here's how to do it:

1. *Identify where you are stuck.* Amanda felt torn about the new opportunity her employer was offering. When you identify where you are stuck, make your answer one succinct sentence—a factual rather than an emotional description of the problem.

2. *Clarify the core issue that has you stuck.* What are the conflicting emotions that tell you you're stuck? For

Amanda, the answer might be, "I feel like I should be excited, but instead I feel guilty."

3. *Ask a question to peel back the layer and get to "why."* Ask, "Why is that?" We could ask Amanda, "What exactly has you feeling guilty and excited?"

4. *Drill down with questions until you get to an iceberg.* Remember, an iceberg is your belief or thought about how things should be. It guides the decisions and actions you take, navigating you almost subconsciously. Ask, "What does that mean? What's the worst part of that? What's most upsetting about that?"

5. *Choose whether to hold on to your iceberg or melt it.* Once you discover an iceberg belief, ask yourself, "Is this helping me or hurting me in this situation? Do I still want to hold on to this belief?"

As Amanda went through this process, she unearthed two deeply held but conflicting beliefs: First, a woman should do all she can to maximize her professional and financial potential. Second, moms who are truly committed step out of the workforce when they have children. With a child on the way, these two icebergs collided. Amanda decided that both beliefs were hurting her to some degree and she needed to edit them. The first because it allowed no leeway to take a break or have different "seasons" of her career, and the second because she felt it too judgmental.

Amanda decided to discard the judgment about whether a mom is committed, acknowledging that not everyone's circumstances are the same. Prayerfully, she modified her iceberg beliefs to these: "When I work, I will work with excellence and take advantage of only those opportunities I sense God leading me to. My professional life must work around my family life." She made the decision to assist with the launch of the new project and talked to her company about a modified work-from-home schedule after her baby. After a few months, she would assess whether her professional life was truly working around her family life or if further changes and sacrifices were needed.

Becoming aware of your thoughts and beliefs, especially conflicting ones, is essential to understanding why you may be stuck and a key to intentional thinking. Your thoughts create your reality.

Get Moving!

What "icebergs" are keeping you stuck? Do you have deeply held beliefs that are preventing you from moving forward? How will you decide to adjust or let them go?

_____

_____

_____

_____

_____

Prayer

God, sometimes I just don't even understand why I get stuck. I stand at an impasse and have no idea what the right answer could be. Yet my instincts tell me there is an answer. There is a reason I'm stuck. Help me peel back the layers so I can clearly see what is holding me back. Where my thoughts are hindering me, replace them with Your thoughts. Give me wisdom and clarity and new understanding that I've never had before. Then show me how to break through the iceberg beliefs that stagnate me so I can move forward. Amen.

Pinpoint Your Fear Pattern

Declaration

Today, I choose courage over fear. I know God has not given me a spirit of fear. I will not respond to life's challenges and opportunities with dread, hesitation, and fear. To overcome fear, I must first acknowledge it exists and then identify the self-sabotaging thoughts that feed it. When I do that, I am empowered to take those thoughts captive and line them up with God's Word and will for my life.

Key Points

- The events of your life do not create your reactions. Your *thoughts* about the events of your life create your reactions.

- Being stuck is a pattern of behavior. If you can identify your pattern, you can devise a plan of action to break the pattern permanently through new habits and thoughts.

Four primary fears are at the core of almost every hesitation, insecurity, doubt, and "stuckness." You have a "primary" fear. Although your challenges in different areas of life may appear unrelated, they are often rooted in one primary fear. Identify your fear pattern and you can uproot the strongholds in your life.

Choose to be self-aware. When I find myself in a scenario in which I am stuck, confused, or paralyzed by fear, I ask, "How else is this fear showing up in my life?" *Seeing* the pattern is my first step to *breaking* the pattern.

Take the Career Clogger Quiz starting on page 197 or online at www.valorieburton.com. There are quizzes for each key area of your life—your relationships, career, health, finances, and spiritual life. Check your primary fears for each area.

Primary Fears in the Five Key Areas of Your Life

What's Your Money Monster (Primary Financial Fear)?

- ☐ Fear of Success
- ☐ Fear of Failure
- ☐ Fear of Disapproval
- ☐ Fear of Losing Control
- ☐ Unstuck and Unstoppable

What's Your Love Lie (Primary Relationship Fear)?

- ☐ Fear of Success
- ☐ Fear of Failure
- ☐ Fear of Disapproval
- ☐ Fear of Losing Control
- ☐ Unstuck and Unstoppable

What's Your Health Hang-up (Primary Health Stumbling Block)?

- ☐ Fear of Success
- ☐ Fear of Failure
- ☐ Fear of Disapproval
- ☐ Fear of Losing Control
- ☐ Unstuck and Unstoppable

What's Your Career Clogger (Primary Fear at Work)?

- ☐ Fear of Success
- ☐ Fear of Failure
- ☐ Fear of Disapproval

- [ ] Fear of Losing Control
- [ ] Unstuck and Unstoppable

What's Your Spiritual Snag (Primary Spiritual Fear)?
- [ ] Fear of Success
- [ ] Fear of Failure
- [ ] Fear of Disapproval
- [ ] Fear of Losing Control
- [ ] Unstuck and Unstoppable

Get Moving!

Did any of your primary fears appear in more than one category? If so, which one and how many times did it appear?

_____

_____

_____

If you have the same primary fear in multiple areas, that fear is your fear pattern. If you do not have the same fear in multiple areas, there is no fear pattern. You can focus on conquering each fear independent of the others.

Prayer

God, Your Word promises that if I lack wisdom about something, I can ask You and You'll give it to me. Open my eyes to any potential patterns of fear that are a snare on my path. Give me the wisdom, faith, and courage to conquer my fears and move forward in faith. Lord, strengthen me to break free from any strongholds that threaten to suck me back into old patterns of behavior. Renew my mind so that my thoughts are aligned with Your thoughts. When negative, self-defeating thoughts come, help me replace them. Amen.

Start Moving and Inspiration Will Come

Declaration

I choose to move toward that to which God is calling me.
I will not wait for a divine miracle to do for me what I can begin
doing myself. I don't have to have all the answers up front.
I just have to have the faith and self-control to get started.
Once I start, the path will begin to unfold.

Key Points

- Getting moving in a physical sense will begin to move you in other important ways.

- Stop waiting for inspiration to move you. Start moving and the inspiration will come.

One of the most common misunderstandings that keeps us stuck is the belief that we need to feel inspired to get started. So we wait for inspiration. We wait to *feel* like moving forward before we move forward. Days, weeks, even months can pass without that feeling showing up, so we stay right where we are. Paired with that idea is often a simultaneous, erroneous belief that the people out there forging ahead—unstoppable in their progress—are somehow more inspired. Well, that is partly right. They *are* more inspired. But not for the reason we insist on believing.

Those who are more inspired didn't get that way because inspiration finds its way to them more often. They are more inspired because they don't wait for inspiration to move them. They understand that if they start moving, the inspiration will come. So they get moving. They start uninspired. They see the work that needs to be done and realize it must be tackled. They must dive in. They don't always *feel* like diving in. They, too, are bombarded by more instant-gratification distractions. However, they have disciplined themselves to not be lured by those distractions—at least not for long.

This single piece of wisdom is worth taping to your desk or using as the background on your laptop or posting somewhere you can be reminded: *Start moving and the inspiration will come.* Keep it in front of you because in the midst of procrastinating, you will surely forget it. You will tell yourself you can't get started because you don't know how. You don't feel moved. You don't feel *anything*.

But what if you stopped telling yourself you need to feel something in particular to get unstuck? What if you embraced the truth that getting unstuck is a choice? It is a decision separate from your feelings. Remember, feelings are honest, but they are not necessarily the truth. In other words, you feel what you feel. I can't tell you what to feel. But feelings are based on your mood and emotions and past experiences and all sorts of stuff that can distort your perception of reality. So whatever you feel today, the truth remains the same: When you start moving, inspiration will come.

Once inspiration comes, the moving will be quick. You will finally *feel* the feelings you want to feel. Not dread or the fear of getting it wrong or failing. Instead, you will feel alive. Passionate. Determined. Hopeful. *Unstoppable.*

Get Moving!

What is the goal you most want to reach at this point in your life? (Consider your health, relationships, finances, career, and spiritual life.)

_____

_____

_____

Why is it important to you?

_____

_____

_____

Why is it important to God?

_____

_____

_____

What specific, measurable, and time-sensitive goals would bring you closer to that vision?

_____

_____

_____

_____

Prayer

Lord, Your Word tells me that when I draw near to You, You draw nearer to me. I believe the same is true when it is time to move forward in faith. As I take action, Your forces rally to my aid and strengthen my efforts. But sometimes I seem to operate just the opposite. I wait for inspiration before I move. I know it is fear. It is procrastination. It is perfectionism. And none of those things is Your will for me. So today, God, help me take a step forward. Right now. Not an hour from now. Not tomorrow. When I start moving forward in faith, inspiration comes. Thank You for what is about to happen as I take a step forward in faith! Amen.

Take Charge of This Moment

Declaration

Today, I claim my power to make a decision and take action. When I am fully present, I can take charge of the moment that is here right now. It is then that I immediately become unstuck! My goal, then, is to become a master of each moment, constantly redirecting my thoughts and energy to the opportunity of the here and now.

Key Points

- You cannot get unstuck yesterday. You can only get unstuck *now*.

- You can train your brain to focus. It takes practice, but it can be done.

I am the master of productive procrastination. The things I manage to get done when there are other, more important things to do can be amazing! I have been known to redesign entire rooms of my house, reconnect with old friends I've been meaning to call for months, and finally launch all sorts of dormant projects while I am supposedly about to dive into that ever-so-important project. The crazy thing is that most of the stuff I get done is stuff I was previously procrastinating about, but now that there is something more pressing and challenging before me, suddenly these old procrastinations look like a breeze. Can you relate?

It is a form of stuckness that really doesn't look to the outside world like you are stuck at all. To the outside world, you are unstoppable. Just look at all the stuff you get done!

Of course, to get unstuck, you have to conquer the productive procrastination habit. If you habitually delay projects, the key is to capture your thoughts. Procrastination is nothing more than a reaction to a "trigger." A trigger is any challenge or stressor in your life that causes a reaction in you. A reaction is either an emotion or (in)action. In between a trigger and a reaction lies a thought.

We don't just move from trigger to reaction, although we often believe that we do. We even talk about it in such a way. "I really need to clean out that closet, but I keep procrastinating." "I knew that paper was due at the end of the semester, but for some reason I always wait until the last possible day to start on it!" Between thinking of cleaning out the closet(trigger) but instead deciding to go to the mall(reaction), you had a thought that diverted your attention. Between "I have a paper to write" (trigger) and waiting until the last day to get started (reaction), you told yourself you had time to spare.

The process of procrastination only happens because of what you say to yourself—often subconsciously. It usually sounds something like this:

- It is too overwhelming. I don't have time to start right now.

- I'm afraid it is going to turn out awful. I'll wait to get started until I know exactly how I want to do this.

- I know it won't be perfect and I'm really dreading the scrutiny.

- I hate doing this. I don't want to do it. I won't do it—well, at least not today.

No wonder you haven't gotten started! If your thoughts are these or something similar, nothing you are saying to yourself would make you want to get started. The key is to pause in the moment when it is time to turn your focus toward the task at hand. Literally, stop. Take a deep breath. Acknowledge your thoughts. Then say to yourself, *These thoughts are not mine. They are not God's. These are self-sabotaging thoughts I need to discard. They are of no use if I am to live the amazing life God imagined for me.* Then, very intentionally, shift your thoughts toward what you want. Ask yourself, "What thoughts might God want me to embrace about this task I am procrastinating on?" "What thoughts will empower and compel me to confidently and passionately move forward?" Your new thoughts might look something like this:

- Moving forward is a sign of standing in authority and divine power for my life.

- I don't have to move forward perfectly. I give myself permission to do this imperfectly—so long as I do it.

- I don't have to like doing this to do it. The sooner I get started, the sooner I will finish what needs to be accomplished—and that will give me freedom.

- I will never gain everyone's approval and I am perfectly okay with that. I refuse to be bound by a fear of people.

- This is not nearly as big of a deal as I am making it. I will break this into bite-sized chunks I can get started with today.

- I am a productive, energetic person. Moving forward is what I do. And when I do it, I become unstoppable!

Get Moving!

To get unstuck, you must learn to master the moment when you are about to move in the wrong direction. You must stop, consciously choose an empowering thought that moves you forward, and go forth in the right direction. Every day, practice this process. Every day, take charge of your moments.

1. Ask yourself, "What action have I delayed?"

2. Take a deep breath.

3. Direct your thoughts toward taking action.

4. Whatever it is, take action—right now. Yes, right this moment.

Prayer

Lord, in this nonstop, wired world, there are so many temptations for distraction. And I admit, I succumb to the temptation a lot. Sometimes, I'm not even sure how to stop procrastinating and multitasking, but I see what that habit is doing to my dreams. I don't move forward—or at least not as much as I would like. I need Your help. Right now, help me take charge of this moment so that I can be productive and effective. Give me the power to step over this hurdle and break through to a life of action. Help me practice daily the art of being fully present and take charge of my moments. Amen.

Stop Rehashing the Past

Declaration

Today, I choose to forget what is behind and press toward what is ahead! I cannot move forward while I'm still looking backward. I trust God that the best is yet to come, but first I must make peace with the past and face forward.

Key Points

- Rehashing negative feelings and situations mires you in stale, ugly old emotions.

- Constantly going over pain from the past is a sign that you are not completely healed from the situation.

- Be proactive about processing your past. Get the help you need to work through it.

It's the place where we got stuck that can be so darn difficult to quit talking about. The ex who did you wrong. The backstabbing coworker who got the promotion. The financial situation that went south. The church member who acted anything but Christlike. We've all been there. You think you've moved on, but one mention of something that reminds you of that old situation and you can spend the next hour rehashing the negativity with the closest listening ear. And so you find yourself dragged back into old feelings, old hurts, and old anger over a situation you thought you were free from. Sometimes this type of rehashing sneaks up on you. You see the gossip train leaving the station and you know you shouldn't run after it, but you do. The lure of rehashing the situation is too strong and you don't resist. Before you know it, you're stuck in the mire of old, stale, ugly emotions.

What past situation do you still rehash? Whose hurtful words do you still repeat to others? Rehashing the past is a sign you are not completely healed from the situation. Forgiveness is still needed. Release is still required. One of the many ways we hang on to the past is by repeatedly recounting the details of it. In some instances, we can revel in it. It is our way of remaining the victim, even if unconsciously. To reclaim your power, you must surrender the situation to God. Let it go. Stop trying so hard to make sense of it. Accept that sometimes things never make sense. Lean not on your own understanding, or you'll find yourself trapped by the desire to figure it all out, psychoanalyze all involved, and get closure when sometimes there never will be any.

As a coach, I often explain the difference between a need for coaching versus a need for therapy in this way: If the topic is like an open wound, and when I touch it you flinch because it still stings, therapy is your best option. If the topic is like a scar and when I touch it, you feel nothing, you're a good candidate for coaching. I see the scar. It shows me you've been through something. But it is completely healed. Even if I pinched it, it wouldn't hurt anymore. And therefore, I don't need to nurse it. Rehashing occurs when the situation at hand has not yet healed. You can't talk about the subject without "nursing it" by discussing all the details and conjuring up negative energy and emotions.

The good news is that you can stop rehashing the past. First, be honest with yourself. Have you processed your past? Have you done the work to heal and forgive and surrender the outcome to God? If not, be proactive. Find a good counselor or therapist. Talk to a wise friend. Get the help it will take to work through it.

Get Moving!

If you truly believe you are over it, then it's time to lay it to rest. Symbolically, you might consider a ceremony of sorts. Try this:

- Write on pieces of paper who or what you need to forgive about the situation.

- Write a list of the lessons you have learned from the situation.
- Pray over each one.

Prayer

Lord, help me stop ruminating on the past. It is so tempting, and too often, I succumb to the temptation. I know that when I spend my time looking back at the past, it is impossible to move forward in a powerful way. Heal me from the wounds of my past so I can be free to step into the amazing life You've imagined for me—a life in which I live in the present and savor the possibilities my future holds. Amen.

Surrender

Today, I choose to surrender everything that makes me anxious,
fearful, and hesitant. I give myself completely to the all-knowing
power of God. I let go of the need to control the outcome of my
efforts, the timing of my desires, and the actions of others.
I know that it is only when I surrender that I am truly free.

Key Points

- The idea of being in control is an illusion.
- Surrender frees you to live fully, let go, and enjoy your
  journey.

Surrender. It is a word that conjures up thoughts of giving up and
giving in. I picture soldiers on the battlefield, rifles above their
heads, allowing all their hard-fought efforts to dissipate, all
they've fought for coming to nothing. It is no wonder then that the
idea of surrendering is not an idea I naturally embrace—even surrendering to God. I have to talk myself into it. I have to remind myself of
the wisdom of surrender.

Sometimes, we find ourselves stuck because we are fighting the
wrong battle—one we will never win because it is not ours to win. We
work ourselves into a frenzy creating plans, devising strategies, and
repeatedly hitting a roadblock. Determined not to give up on the goal,
we go back to the drawing board and come up with a new plan. Surely,
this plan will work. We've learned from our mistakes, accounted for
them, and sought advice from all the right people. We try again. And

once again, we hit a roadblock. This cycle can go for some time before we get so worn down we even secretly question whether God is on our side. Have you ever been there?

It isn't something I pride myself on admitting as a believer—the idea that I have ever questioned God. But I have. I have had my moments—quiet moments—lying in bed pondering a situation and wondering why God was withholding something from me. In those moments, I tick off my list of good deeds, my track record of obedience to God's guidance in the face of fear, and recount the Scriptures that fill me with hope:

> With God all things are possible (Matthew 19:26).

> I can do all this through him who gives me strength (Philippians 4:13).

> Take delight in the LORD, and he will give you the desires of your heart (Psalm 37:4).

> To him who is able to do immeasurably more than all we ask or imagine, according to his power that is at work within us, to him be glory (Ephesians 3:20-21).

I replay those Scriptures in my mind and I begin to wonder why they aren't working for me. Am I being punished for something? What am I doing wrong? Why does it seem to happen so easily for so-and-so, but not for me? And as I ponder more, the temptation is to become angry. Instead, I grow curious. I've walked long enough with God to know those questions are the wrong ones to ask. I've been humbled frequently enough to know my good deeds and obedience fall short of deserving even the blessings that have already overtaken me. Those questions are the enemy's whisper, not God's. In moments of deep disappointment and frustration, when I lean on my own understanding rather than trusting God's process, my ears are open to hear the lies. It is a line of thinking that gets me stuck, asking, "Why? Why don't You know better what I need? Why don't You see the timeline I see? Why don't You open the door that would be so easy for You to open?"

Rather than look at such questions rhetorically, I believe God invites us to actually answer the questions. I mean, He is God. And there must be an answer, right? And if He truly loves us, there must be a reason your timing and God's timing aren't aligned—an explanation for that closed door.

Spiritual surrender is to stop fighting for your own agenda and turn yourself over to the service of the Almighty. It is to want what God wants for you. It is to stop battling with Him and ask, "Lord, what are You trying to show me? What are You trying to teach me? How do You want to use me?" There is a reason the door isn't open. But in our finite understanding, we may never know the answer why. Our alternative is to keep fighting, to keep pushing against circumstances that push back with equal or greater strength—and remain stuck. Or we can throw our hands up in courageous trust of the Lord. When we do that, we are no longer stuck. We are no longer pushing against what *is*. Instead, we rest in God's arms and flow in His plan. We find the good in what He has given us and trust that He knows best. We breathe. We trust Him. We surrender.

Why are we trying so hard to figure everything out?

Do not be wise in your own eyes (Proverbs 3:7).

I vividly recall one afternoon in late 1999 when my mind was spinning with excitement at the possibilities of pursuing my purpose wholeheartedly. The questions in my head were coming more rapidly than I could possibly answer them. *When could you sell enough books to do this full time? What would that take? What will you do with your public relations business? Who could manage it for you? How much money would you need? What about your clients? Will they stick around if you are not managing their accounts? How will you travel and speak and keep up with all that you have to do in this business? What if you focused first on growing that business so you can sell it and then do what you really want to do for a living?*

Are you getting tired just reading all these questions? I bet you are.

So just imagine how tired I was getting trying to answer them! The truth is, I couldn't answer them. At least not right in that moment. But as I drove down McKinney Avenue that day in uptown Dallas, my mind was on everything but the road. My blood pressure was rising. My shoulders were tense. My breath was shallow. And I was trying to figure it all out.

But...

> Trust in the LORD with all your heart
> and lean not on your own understanding;
> in all your ways submit to him,
> and he will make your paths straight.
>   (Proverbs 3:5-6)

Let me say part of that again: Lean not on your own understanding. Trying to figure things out without God's input is a sure way to get stuck and remain stuck. Intelligence and perfectionism can get you many things, but unstuck is not one of them. Those who consider themselves especially smart can be tempted to believe more in their own ability to figure things out than in God's ability to come through for them. As smart as I thought I was, I simply could not see the big picture. It was not time yet to know all of the answers.

Shoot, I still don't know all the answers! It can be so easy to demand we know the answers before we take another step forward. In reality, such a demand shows our lack of faith.

Such was the case for me. As I pondered rapid-fire questions that day, I came to an intelligent and logical conclusion: I would grow my business over the next few years and get it to the point where I could sell it and be financially independent enough to finally pursue God's calling on my life. "That's it!" I thought. "I just need to dig my heels in and make this happen."

Just as I said that to myself, I heard the voice of the Holy Spirit interrupt. "Ahem." He cleared His throat. "Nope, that's not what you're going to do."

"I'm not?" I responded.

"No, you're not," He confirmed. "Let Me tell you something. You will never make more money doing anything other than what I called you to do."

He didn't promise money would come quickly. He didn't promise how much money would come. But He made it clear to me that following His promptings would lead to more success than anything I could do on my own. He interrupted me to let me know that all my strategizing and worrying had led me to a plan of action that was less than His plan for me.

The Bible asks us to trust God and lean not on our own understanding. When we do so, God will guide us. That means we have to have the faith to believe He will. We have to let go of the need to control. We have to push past our fear.

Get Moving!

What plan(s) are you creating without God's input?

_____

_____

_____

_____

_____

Write out a prayer asking the Holy Spirit for His wisdom in your specific situation.

_____

_____

_____

_____

_____

_____

Prayer

Your will be done, not mine, Lord. Your will is what I want because Your will is the perfect plan for my life. I ask You to come into my heart right now, God, and make Your desires for me my desires. I want to want what You want. Help me stop fighting for my way and trust that Your plan for me will unfold in the right timing with the right people in the right way. I cannot see what You see, but I can choose right now to trust You with all my heart. Help me surrender each day to You, Lord, focused on knowing that You have me in the palm of Your hand. Help me live in the place of knowing that if it is meant to be, it will divinely unfold. All I have to do is what You ask of me. You will do the rest. I choose right now to accept and embrace Your will, peacefully and contentedly. Amen.

Give Yourself Permission to Do It Badly

Declaration

Today, I choose progress over perfection. I have permission to move forward even if that means I don't know all the answers upon the first step. Fear uses perfection as an excuse for remaining stuck. Faith doesn't require perfection, but action.

Key Points

- Perfection and procrastination are intertwined. Let go of the need for perfection and you are free to move forward.

- When starting a project in which you've been stuck, be willing to do something badly. Just get started. You can go back later and make changes.

- Allow yourself the freedom to make mistakes.

Many years ago, I heard an author tell an interviewer who asked how he became such a prolific writer. "I let myself write badly," he commented. "I don't edit myself—that's for later. I just give myself permission to write whatever comes and then I have no excuse for not writing."

It was a profound statement. So often, we get stuck because we are deathly afraid of not being perfect. But why is perfection needed? It isn't. What are you holding off on because the circumstances have not lined up in the way you think they must?

_____

_____

_____

What good are you withholding from yourself as a sort of punishment for not getting it right? What gems are you keeping to yourself until you perfect them? What purpose are you not fulfilling because you believe your skills are not honed enough?

I'd like to ask you today to adjust your standards. Notice I didn't say, "Have low standards." If you must meet an unreachable standard before you even get started—for example, having the intricate details of your plan completely worked out—you will likely never start. In fact, you might need to ask yourself whether your sky-high standards are really just fear in disguise. If you can't get started because it isn't all figured out, then you never have to discover just how good you really are. You might have to face disappointment. You might get rejected. Maybe you'll discover you're not as great as you thought you were.

These assessments may sound harsh, but the brain has a way of avoiding pain, even if the actions are subconscious. For perfectionists, who are expert controllers, the idea of an outcome that is less than ideal must be avoided at all costs. But such an attitude is not godly. It requires no faith. It is bound in fear. Here's the real question you need to answer: What if *perfect* is not the goal? What if what you are trying to do does not call for perfection? What if God is waiting on you to stop trying to do it perfectly? The truth is, He doesn't need your perfection—because quite frankly, none of us are. So why do we get stuck, afraid to move forward because everything isn't just right?

I believe it is because the enemy wants to keep us distracted from the real goal. Perfection is elusive. And even when, in our ego, we believe we have achieved it, we are deceived. Perfection lies in imperfection. It lies in the grace to be human, to err, to try again—or not. Think about that project or dream you've been holding off on pursuing or finishing. What would happen if you just rested in God's grace and moved forward imperfectly?

_____

_____

_____

What would happen if you let go of the belief that things must look a certain way in order for you to be happy?

_____

_____

_____

Move from Perfection to Purpose

Hillary Rettig, author of the book *The 7 Secrets of the Prolific: The Definitive Guide to Overcoming Procrastination, Perfectionism, and Writer's Block,* has identified five major characteristics of perfectionists:*

- Defining success narrowly and unrealistically; punishing oneself harshly for perceived failures. A perfectionist perceives her outcomes as being worse than they really are.

- Grandiosity—the deluded idea that things that are difficult for other people should be easy for you.

- Shortsightedness, manifested in a "now or never" or "do or die" attitude.

- Overidentification with work. When things are going well, a perfectionist feels like king or queen of the world, and if they fail, he or she is down in the dumps.

---

* Hillary Rettig, "Perfectionism Defined," June 2013, www.hillaryrettig.com/perfectionism.

- Overemphasis on product (vs. process) and on external rewards.

The goal God wants us to focus on is not perfection, but purpose. When we free ourselves to take steps forward, even if the steps are wobbly or just plain bad, we allow Him to use and teach us in greater ways. There is often far more learning that occurs in doing things wrong than in doing them right. When God says *move*, obedience is the only act of faith. He knows our weaknesses. He knows our shortcomings. So if it is time to move, surely He has a purpose for prompting you to move. Rather than holding out for perfection, step out for purpose. Keep your heart and spirit open to discerning your next step.

Remember: You do not have permission to tell God *no* just because you feel inadequate for the task at hand.

Get Moving!

In what way(s) are you demanding perfection before you move forward? What would happen if you moved forward anyway?

_____

_____

_____

_____

_____

_____

_____

Prayer

Lord, give me courage, lots of courage. When I hesitate out of perfectionism, help me remember that You are a God of purpose and that if You tell me to move, the only perfect action is living in accordance with Your will for me. I want to move when You say move. So today, Lord, I give myself permission to do it imperfectly, knowing Your grace is sufficient for me. Amen.

Commit or Quit

Declaration

Today, I choose to commit to my goals wholeheartedly, knowing it might not be easy, but it will be worth it. I will inevitably deal with obstacles, fear, and inconveniences on the way to the goal. The only way to reach it is to commit with passion and be willing to make sacrifices. If I'm not ready to do that, I'm not ready for the goal.

Key Points

- Get serious about your dream.
- Sometimes you have to *give* up to *go* up.

During a conference call I hosted recently for aspiring life and business coaches, I invited several successful coaches to share their "secrets" to excelling in the field. One of the coaches, my friend and author Marshawn Evans, made a profound point. You must find the resources to invest in training that will empower you to move toward your dream—in this case, one caller's dream of becoming a life coach. I think it is a point that is relevant to us all no matter what the goal. "We find a way to do what is important to us," she said. "Many of us have bought things that are lying around the house that we never use that cost more than the investment it would take to get our dream off the ground."

As I pondered this point, I realized it is true. Of course, there are times when getting serious so we can accomplish our priorities may take longer than we'd like. But whether your priority is getting out of debt, making an important transition, or following your dream, it begins with a decision that your dream is a priority. And if it is a priority, you must be intentional about investing in what it takes to bring that dream to life.

What is your dream right now? I don't know about you, but I have found that my life's biggest dreams have never come cheaply. They've taken a lot of effort and time. They've required risks that scared the heck out of me. I moved forward with my knees shaking, not knowing what the future would hold, but hoping in faith that God would be with me whatever the answer. And my dreams have usually required a financial investment—like going back to school at 34 years old to an Ivy League university, and not on a scholarship! But there is not one dream I've pursued that I regretted.

Whatever your dream, commit to it on a whole new level. Know that it will take some sacrifice. Get creative about finding the time, the money, or other resources you'll need. Get serious about making it happen. Get brave about trusting God is with you if you follow the desires of your heart. Don't expect it to be easy. Just expect it to be worth it.

Janet was always talking about how much she wanted to get out of her stressful job. She hated it. She didn't like the firm she worked for. She complained about company ethics, about her boss, about her coworkers. And she had a plan to take the leap: a well-thought-out consulting business she'd been working on for three years. In fact, she now generated a consistent part-time income from the business. She'd stashed the part-time income away to invest in marketing her services when she was ready to take the leap. She had a savings cushion most people would envy—two years of living expenses plus her retirement savings. She had no debt.

Over the years, she had carefully outlined a plan for when she would be ready to step out on faith, and she'd now reached the benchmark. But something was wrong. She was afraid her savings weren't enough. She realized she could make it and she'd probably land a few more clients soon after going into business full-time, but giving up the guarantee of a regular salary was cause for hesitation.

"I've worked really hard to move toward my dream," she admitted. "But now that I'm prepared, I am afraid I'll never make as much money working for myself as I'm making in my current job."

"Really?" I probed. "Not even after a few years?"

She pondered the question for a moment. "It would take a lot of resources to get there," she acknowledged. "And an awful lot of energy. I mean, I work hard now, but I also have a lot of resources and support at work and that will all be gone. I guess the reality of my dream is sinking in now that it's time to take a step forward."

"What would it mean to you to never make as much money again?" I asked.

"It would mean I'm giving up something I worked extremely hard to get. I didn't just ascend to this position. I had to really fight hard for it. There were people who didn't want me to get here, who intentionally tried to sabotage my ability to get a promotion. It's been a long road. And I finally have the respect I always wanted."

We often think the grass is greener on the other side. Get clear about how much you want your dream. Goal-setting researchers point out that one of the most important elements of successful goal-setting is commitment. It may sound simple, but if you are not truly committed to the goal you are unlikely to reach it. Obstacles will come. Difficulties will test your tenacity. Unless you are committed, you won't weather the inevitable storms.

Sometimes, what looks like being stuck is really a lack of commitment to a goal. It appears to be indecisiveness or fear or overanalysis. A more accurate label is "uncommitted." Get honest with yourself. Remember, truth is your most powerful tool for getting unstuck. Answer these questions to gauge your commitment:

On a scale of 1 to 10, how committed are you to your vision? _____

What sacrifices would you be willing to make to ensure your goal is realized?

_____

_____

_____

At what point will you feel you have sacrificed too much and it is time to abandon the goal?

_____

_____

_____

Get Moving!

When it comes to a goal or dream that really matters to you, be creative and persistent about finding the resources to take the next step.

What excuse have you made for why you cannot have your dream? If you were to let go of that excuse, what would you have to do to make it happen? Are you serious enough about your dream to do that now?

_____

_____

_____

_____

_____

_____

Prayer

God, give me the boldness and courage to commit wholeheartedly to living an amazing life. Help me run with open arms toward the goals You place in my heart—committed to the journey, the wait, and pressing through the inevitable challenges that will appear. Increase my tenacity. Infuse me with perseverance. And help me be decisive when the right answer is to change course and let go of something that is not in Your will for me. Make it clear, God. Amen.

Today Is a Day You Can Win

Declaration

I choose to embrace today as a fresh opportunity to move forward. Even if yesterday was just plain awful and I was at my worst, I choose right now to forgive myself, let it go, and make the best of the day in front of me. I will set a goal I can accomplish today and I will choose joy in the process. If I am facing the wrong direction, I choose to pivot toward the right one. If I have struggled with procrastination, today I choose to take action. Today is a new day!

Key Points

- Make a game out of getting unstuck. Lightening it up makes it fun and easier.

- Before you go to bed (and certainly before you get out of bed in the morning), identify what a "win" looks like for the upcoming day.

- "Play" triggers positive emotions that inspire creativity and productivity.

Hoping to inspire me on a day when I found myself in a rut, my husband texted me a statement he thought might motivate me: "Today is a day you can win!"

I was overwhelmed at that very moment and this little ditty didn't make me feel any better. In fact, I was so frustrated at the time that I couldn't even figure out what he was talking about. Admittedly, sometimes I'm a little too literal.

"Huh?" I texted back.

"I just thought of it," he shot back. "Life is like a game. Every day you wake up, you get a new shot to do better. You might have lost yesterday, but today you can win!" He was genuinely inspired by the thought. I was not—at first.

"Okay," I said, wallowing in my stress. "Thanks for trying to motivate me."

I know, I didn't respond well. But have you ever had one of those days when you are overwhelmed and someone who cares tries to encourage you and it just doesn't quite do the trick? You appreciate the sentiment, but with the flood of stress and pressure you feel, your attitude needs an adjustment. That was where I was. Even so, I was intrigued enough to bring it back up the next day.

"You know yesterday when you said, 'Today is a day you can win'?" I started. "I realized the thought of trying to win a game every day made me feel more stressed. I just didn't feel inspired by that idea. I feel like I'm always striving to win and sometimes, what I really want is just a break from stacking up another win."

"Hmph," he said, curiously. "Well, you don't have to play every day. But you can use the game when it suits you. It can make your day more fun. It gives you an aim. Take the game out when it suits you, and put it away when it doesn't. When you play Monopoly, you know what moves you need to make to get ahead. You can do the same thing with your day."

My wheels began to turn. *I could stand to lighten up about my deadlines,* I thought. *I mean, the stuff I'm working on is actually fun. Maybe hubby's on to something.* Later that week, I woke up and my first thought was, "What would it take for me to win today?" I identified just two actions I needed to take that would make me feel the day was a "win." I smiled. I felt good. *I like this game,* I thought.

When you are stuck, it is often because the moves you need to make feel burdensome and heavy. Seeing the moves as a part of a bigger game—a game that offers you the opportunity to be unstoppable—can make it feel lighter. Think of it as the "Amazing Life" game. You can play every day if you want. It's not hard to win. You just need to understand the rules and get in the game. When it come to being unstoppable, the rules are simple.

Game Rules

The game is a game of fear versus faith. Fear's goal is to defeat your destiny and undermine your purpose on the planet. Your goal is to use your toolbox of love, faith, courage, and boldness to overcome the fear and the obstacles, distractions and pitfalls that are thrown your way in the form of frustrating people, bad choices, rejection, failure, expectations, pressures, insecurities, irritations, illnesses, poor planning, disappointments, and even traumas and tragedies.

Rule #1: Prayerfully identify one to three things that must happen in a given day in order to win. These "moves" define success for that day. On some days, the moves might include a major project or a conversation that needs to take place. On other days, a clearly defined goal may be something more subjective, such as to do something kind for at least one person or feel relaxed and at peace throughout the day. The moves are up to you.

Rule #2: You will get sidetracked, distracted, shot down, and even tripped up by your own mistakes and inaction. You cannot give up. Instead, you must get up. Three steps forward, two steps back. That's okay. Stumbling is inevitable. Don't let it shock you. It doesn't matter how long it takes you to get back up and on track. As long as you get up, you win.

Rule #3: Every move in the right direction earns you double points in this game. You will be repeatedly enticed to stay right where you are—to remain stagnant, not grow, and even lose ground instead of gaining it. Stay focused and you will win.

Rule #4: Stretching earns you triple points. You will be stretched beyond your comfort zone. You must keep moving despite your discomfort. You win when your comfort zone expands. When your comfort zone expands, you enlarge your territory—and your influence. Your faith will embolden others—family members, kids, coworkers, and others in your sphere of influence—to stretch their faith, too.

Rule #5: You must stop at each milestone and savor the rewards of your labor! If you miss this step, you can't win the game.

This is a game you can win. When you need a break from it, "put it back on the shelf," as my husband told me. If play comes naturally to you, this motivator will be a welcome addition to your toolkit. If play doesn't come so naturally, it's a chance for you expand your horizons, try something new, and lighten your approach to getting unstuck.

When my husband took the VIA Character Strengths assessment to learn his strengths, his #1 strength turned out to be "humor and playfulness." When he took the happiness test from my book *Happy Women Live Better* (www.happywomantest.com), not surprisingly, the results revealed his #1 personal happiness trigger is "play." Making a game of just about anything comes naturally for him. And games motivate him because play is just a part of who he is. For me, on the other hand, play is neither a top strength (not even in my top 15!) or a personal happiness trigger (in my bottom 4). I'm working on this—no pun intended!

Get Moving!

Today is a day you can win. You can make the right moves that empower you to move a step in the right direction. Answer this question for yourself right now:

In the upcoming day, what moves will you need to make in order to win your "Amazing Life" game? Identify only one to three moves. In this game, you don't win by overwhelming yourself! Keep your list manageable. Set yourself up to win.

Move #1:

_____

_____

_____

Move #2 (optional):

_____

_____

_____

Move #3 (optional)

_____

_____

_____

Prayer

Lord, thank You that each day is a new opportunity to be unstoppable. Thank You for the grace to make mistakes, start again, get stuck, and fight my way forward. Thank You for Your promise that the righteous may stumble, but they will not utterly fall because You will uphold them with Your hand. God, what moves do You want me to make today? Make it clear. Then empower me with the tenacity, persistence, and energy to take action. And help me have fun while I'm at it! For I know Your joy is my strength. Amen.

Stop Catastrophizing!

Declaration

Today I choose to notice the irrational, negative thoughts that cause me to jump from zero to "everybody's dead" in 2.5 seconds! Before I follow the thought into a counterproductive place that leaves me feeling anxious, afraid, and unproductive, I will stop and ask, "Is this a God thought?" If not, it's got to stop.

Key Points

- Letting your imagination run out of control can cause needless anxiety, drama, and wasted energy.

- Ask yourself if your negative self-talk is helping you or harming you.

- Rather than obsessing over miseries that may never arise, imagine a future that's worth moving toward.

It was five minutes past her son's curfew when Angela glanced at the clock. When she called her sixteen-year-old son, Derrick, on his cell phone and got his voicemail, Angela's thoughts went straight to a scary scenario: *What if Derrick ran the car off the road and he's dead? And some looters stole his wallet? And they can't identify him, so they don't know to call me? And he hit someone's car and that person died too and the family is going to sue us, so now we'll be broke and childless?*

We can dismiss Angela's thought as crazy—or we can admit that we have all had moments when our imagination spiraled out of control. Psychologists even have a name for it: *catastrophizing*.

If you don't catastrophize, you may live or work with someone who does. Although it sounds like a harmless quirk, it can cause a lot of anxiety, wasted energy, and drama. A few years back, I gathered some ideas on catastrophizing from a former professor of mine. Karen Reivich, Ph.D., is the author of *The Resilience Factor*. I used her ideas to create a four-step plan you can use to rein in your thoughts before (and even after) they nose-dive into negativity and get stuck there.

1. Catch yourself in the act. When you're feeling anxious, notice what you say to yourself. When that thought first hits, ask yourself, "And then what will happen?" Keep asking yourself that question until you unearth your greatest fear. Bingo—that's your worst-case scenario.

2. Once you spot your big fear, ask yourself, "Are my thoughts helping me or hurting me right now?" Forcing yourself to stop and answer this question can help you see the urgency of changing your train of thought.

3. Snap out of your spiral by imagining the opposite. What's the best-case irrational scenario of what's about to happen? This is actually fun. For example, imagine that your teen is late getting home because he stopped to help a car accident victim. Your son then saved the man's life and his wife gave your son a lottery ticket to show her gratitude. Lo and behold, he won a million bucks! He'll be home in five minutes with the good news. Irrational? Yes, but much better than the dead-with-no-ID scenario you had a couple minutes before.

4. Ask yourself what's most likely to happen. You've now cleared the way to tell yourself what's most logical: "My son lost track of time, his cell phone battery went dead, and he'll be home in a few minutes. Oh, and he'll be in trouble too." In fact, that's exactly what happened in Angela's real-life scenario.

Of course, bad events sometimes befall us, but writer Mark Twain put it best: "I've lived through some terrible things in my life—some of which actually happened." So rather than obsessing over miseries that may never arise, use that vivid imagination to design a future that's worth moving toward.

Get Moving!

Describe a time when you "catastrophized." Did your worst-case scenario actually come to pass?

_____

_____

_____

_____

_____

Describe a time when you chose to assume the best. What would it take for you to do the same when facing future challenges?

_____

_____

_____

_____

_____

Prayer

Lord, when my negative thoughts begin to spiral out of control into irrational scenarios of all that might go wrong, help me interrupt my thought pattern and change it to something more productive and faith-filled. Make me more aware of the scenarios I allow to play out in my mind that create anxiety and fear and hesitation. Show me all the ways in which I routinely catastrophize and give me hope when I'm tempted to allow my thoughts to spiral downward. I know that as I think, so am I. Today, help me direct my thoughts rather than allowing my thoughts to direct me. Amen.

Go Through the Green Lights

Declaration

Today, I choose to notice the doors God opens for me, even when they are not the doors I was trying to open. I trust God to direct my path. Sometimes that means pivoting in a direction that doesn't line up with my plans, but does line up with His.

Key Points

- Listen closely for God's will. Sometimes He makes it obvious through the doors He opens.

- Test whether the doors are divine by lining them up against the Word of God.

I believe in the power of a clear, compelling vision. But what if your vision is clear and compelling, but the doors are opening in a slightly different direction? That very scenario happened to me recently. I created purposeful projects to "go after," yet unrelated opportunities seemed to be consuming my time and making it hard to focus on the "vision."

One morning last week, during my quiet time, I found myself praying about my vision when I sensed a distinct nudge—I believe it was the Holy Spirit. "Valorie, go through the green lights. You keep staring at the red lights waiting for them to turn green for *your* vision when I've stopped traffic and turned the light green for you to move toward *My vision for you*." Wow.

You can be so specific about what you think your dream should look like that you miss the opportunities unfolding right in front of you. I invite you to notice the "green lights" in your life—positive, open doors that welcome you, even though they may not look exactly as you pictured in your vision. Whether an unexpected career opportunity that has the potential to expand your skill set or a "funny Valentine" whose heart and spirit are in exactly the right place, pay attention to the green lights.

In Matthew 11:30 Jesus says, "My yoke is easy and my burden is light." When you live within your purpose, even the most challenging tasks are not burdensome. You may work hard, but deep down you feel energized and gratified by your intense efforts.

Green lights are good opportunities. They are purposeful. But they require you to open your mind and expand your concept of "your" vision.

Get Moving!

I challenge you to pay attention today to the "green lights" and open your mind to following them.

What are you trying to do that has begun to feel burdensome? What "green light" exists in your life that may be a divinely orchestrated opportunity you've taken for granted? What do you view as a distraction that, in fact, is exactly where you are supposed to focus?

Prayer

I don't know why, God, but sometimes I get stuck because I make my path more difficult than it needs to be. I have my idea what it should look like, and when opportunities deviate from that path, I don't always realize that it is You saying, "Come this way." Help me be open to the idea that my path may move in a direction I wasn't expecting—and that direction could be exceedingly better than anything I ever imagined. Rather than pushing against closed doors, help me notice, appreciate, and move toward the doors You open for me. Help me go through the green lights, Lord, where the burden is light and the yoke easy. Amen.

Don't Let the Stuff You Can't Control Control You

Declaration

When I fall into the trap of believing that I must have a particular thing/person/status in order to be happy or successful, I make it an idol. Idol worship creates a trap that keeps me stuck. But I have the power to free myself by tearing down the idols in my life. I can want something and work hard to attain it without allowing the possession of it to dictate my emotions, my worth, or my happiness.

Key Points

- When the doors you want to open simply won't, God will always slip a message under the door. Look down and pick it up.

- Choose to have a healthy detachment from your personal goals. Desire achievements, but don't let your achievements define you.

- When God is the goal, all your other goals are put into proper context.

The first time I bought my own place, a friend came with me as I did some real estate hunting. I could tell she was excited for me, but fascinated too by the prospect of owning a home. "Why don't you consider buying a place of your own?" I asked.

"Oh, no," she said, quickly batting down the idea. "I've just always daydreamed about buying my first home with a husband. The idea of doing it all by myself just wouldn't be as great."

At the time, she didn't have even the prospect of a husband. "Well, what if you don't get married for a long time? You can always buy another house once you get married," I suggested.

"No, no. I'd loved to, but I'm not brave like you. I just feel like that's something I should do with a man," she said.

Her attitude is certainly not unusual. But it illustrates something many of us do: put life on hold until the "right" circumstances arrive—circumstances over which we have no control. It is one thing if God tells you to wait. It is another entirely when your ideals get you stuck. When you look at your relationships or career or finances, in what way(s) does your ideal of success tie your hands and keep you from pursuing the desires of your heart?

Suzanne is a talented vocalist. Her voice could rival just about any popular singer today. She has spent nearly ten years pursuing her dream of a singing career, spending most of those years in Los Angeles, where she has made some headway. She writes and records her own songs, but has also given her own unique twist on covers of classics. But she is beginning to lose heart. Over the last four years, she has come close to getting a big record deal more times than she wants to count. Each time it looks like she's "in," something happens and the deal doesn't materialize. An executive thinks she needs more personality or a different look or suggests she make a few changes to her songs and come back. By the time she makes changes, their interests change or other obstacles pop up.

She's got the look, the talent, and the sound. It seems like a no-brainer. But she's chosen an industry that is among the most competitive on the planet. And even if she does get her big break, there's no guarantee of a hit. Even if there is a hit, there's no guarantee of another hit, let alone a long career. In the meantime, she has only taken jobs that allow her the flexibility to pursue her dream—jobs that will pay the bills, but don't lead to much of a career. Not a career she's interested in, anyway. She hasn't established roots where she lives.

In fact, she's moved quite a bit. She'd love a love life, but she hasn't had time. Meanwhile, the clock is ticking and she is beginning to lose motivation.

Her entire life has centered around one goal: making it as an entertainer. She has sacrificed *everything* for that goal—relationships, financial reward, a permanent home of her own, stability. All of those areas of her life are on hold until it comes together. There is just one major problem: With no clear path to it "coming together" and no guarantees, she risks forgoing success in other areas of life on the chance that her dream materializes. She's stuck. Well, unless she stops allowing the stuff she can't control (when the "big break" happens) to control her.

"I guess I just never thought it would take this long," she said. "I just thought I would pursue my dream and my dream would happen eventually—like, within a few years. I never entertained the idea that I would be ten years into the process and doubting whether it will ever happen. Never."

Have you ever been there? You see the vision. You take that leap of faith. But God's timeline and yours just don't align. As you hold your breath for the vision to come to fruition, you also hold back on other important dreams in your heart. You believed God had an amazing plan for your life, and you thought it was the path you were pursuing. Just because it hasn't unfolded the way *you* thought it should does not mean you were on the wrong path. You can rest in the knowledge that all things *will* work together for good—even when they don't come together in your timing. It could mean that:

- Your vision and definition of success differ from God's.
- Your path was a learning laboratory as God was preparing you for something more or different.
- You are focusing more on the attainment of the goal than on what God is trying to develop in you on the path to your goal.

Balancing Contentment with Desire

The most resilient people are also flexible people. They have a healthy detachment from their goals, meaning they are able to balance contentment with desire. As the apostle Paul wrote in Philippians 4:12-13, "I know what it is to be in need, and I know what it is to have plenty. I have learned the secret of being content in any and every situation, whether well fed or hungry, whether living in plenty or in want. I can do all this through him who gives me strength."

We get stuck when we insist that our circumstances look a certain way. It is a myth that our happiness is determined by what happens. Quite the contrary. It is largely determined by the everyday choices we make—the attitude we choose and the ability to not attach ourselves too strongly to any particular outcome to dictate our happiness. Instead, with our eyes focused on God as the goal, we can go where He wants us to go, give our very best, and trust Him for the outcome.

If you find yourself putting your life on hold while you wait for the exact circumstances to unfold, give yourself permission to release that hold. Open yourself to the adventure that is waiting when you let go of what you think your life *should* be and embrace what it *could* be.

When Your Goal Becomes an Idol

Without realizing it, your goal or dream or the circumstances you desire in your life can become an idol. How do you know if it's an idol? If the following boxes apply, it just might be: Read each one and be brutally honest in your answers.

- ☐ You put the goal (and anyone who has attained the goal) on a pedestal.

- ☐ You believe your achievement of the goal will make you more special, valuable, or worthy in some way.

- ☐ You spend more time trying to attain the goal than you do ensuring you are carrying out your divine purpose in life.

- ☐ If you knew it would guarantee you achieve the goal, you would be willing to stretch the truth or cheat if you wouldn't get caught, lose a relationship, or do something you wouldn't want others to know about.

☐ If the divine nudges you sense in your spirit about the goal don't line up with what you want, you have simply ignored the nudges.

☐ You pursue the goal to the detriment of your relationships, your health, and hopes and dreams you know are divinely inspired.

Get Moving!

It's time to make God the goal. Answer these questions.

What goal or circumstance have you put on such a pedestal that other areas of your life are neglected while you wait?

_____

_____

_____

Name all the ways you can think of that this decision has caused you to put aspects of your life on hold—aspects that God is calling you to nurture and nourish.

_____

_____

_____

Give yourself permission in this moment to ponder the idea of letting the goal go. What would it look like to surrender the outcome of your dream to God?

_____

_____

_____

What would you be able to take off hold if you took the goal off of a pedestal?

_____

_____

_____

    If the idea of changing your goal or taking your life off hold before you reach the goal is so uncomfortable that negative emotions are welling up for you as you answer these questions, then just know that your path has crossed this page at this moment for a purpose. God cares about the desires of your heart (Psalm 37:4). He wants to use you in amazing ways. He also wants to be the first goal in your life. Take a moment now to meditate and listen for the message He is offering you in this moment.

Prayer

Lord, help me avoid putting parts of my life on hold, holding my breath for my desires to manifest before I move forward. You know the desires of my heart. Help me keep from making those desires into idols. Release any strongholds that threaten to divert me from Your path for me. Help me focus on You as the goal. Grow me as I face disappointments. Encourage me as I wait patiently and work toward the goal in Your timing. I don't want to be controlled by the things I can't control. I surrender my desires to You. I trust Your timing. Now show me what You want me to take off hold. Give me the strength and attitude to move forward with joy, confidence, and power. Amen.

Drop the Toxic Friendship

Declaration

I choose my friends intentionally, not by happenstance. Friends can boost my energy or drain it. Iron sharpens iron. My goal is to be iron and attract iron. Sometimes that means making the hard choice of distancing myself from those whose presence is more likely to keep me stuck than propel me forward.

Key Points

- Clearly define your personal criteria for developing a friendship.
- Attitudes are contagious—whether good or bad. Your choice of friends is a major decision on your path to success.

Whose name do you dread seeing pop up on your caller ID? Whose smile seems a little forced when you share your latest success? And who is the *last* person you'd call if you needed to get a secret off your chest? We often use the term *friend* loosely, so I want to encourage you to get clear about who your real friends are and find the courage to cut off those toxic friendships that are draining your spirit and your energy.

Research shows that over the last 25 years, the number of people the average American calls a close confidant has been cut in half—and those people are more likely than ever to be a family member. People who have at least three or four very close friendships are more healthy and more engaged in their jobs, according to research by Gallup. But it's not just about close friendships, but healthy ones. Stressful relationships are detrimental to your well-being, so choose wisely.

When my client Stephanie mentioned her friend Angela, I could hear the stress in her voice. Angela seemed to use Stephanie as her personal crutch for every crisis but never returned the favor—and there was always a crisis, even as far back as high school. One summer, Stephanie drove Angela to work every day for nearly three months without Angela even once offering gas money. Stephanie was resentful, but never said anything. Recently, it was a breakup—the fourth boyfriend in a year—but Stephanie listened agreeably to Angela's complaining and blaming, chiming in with the occasional, "He did what? Oh no he didn't!"

Now, Angela was in a "crisis" at work. Her boss gave her a poor review, citing Angela's poor communication skills with coworkers and moody behavior as a hindrance to her advancement at the company. She was contemplating leaving the job and wanted Stephanie to help her get a position at her company—something Stephanie knew would be disastrous. With professional consequences at stake, she finally mustered the courage to have a heart-to-heart with Angela.

Truth be told, Angela was jealous and she felt entitled to Stephanie's pity and help. Stephanie has a job she loves, a stable, happy love life, and she's loyal—to a fault. Can you relate?

Take care of yourself by being intentional about your friendships. Healthy ones will help you build a foundation for a happier life. Coach yourself with these questions to help you discover who your true friends are—and start nurturing those friendships.

Does the friendship energize me or drain me?

Ideally, your friendships energize you. They bring out your best. If you have to give yourself a mental pep talk before you spend time with someone, it's a big red flag that something's not right. Either have a heart-to-heart about what's not working for you or make a decision to distance yourself from the friendship.

Can I trust this person?

There's no such thing as a friend you can't trust. If you can't trust her, she's not your friend. So stop calling her that. Come up with another name. Associate. Acquaintance. Someone you know. But *not* friend.

Do I like this person?

It sounds obvious, but people become friends with others for all sorts of reasons—convenience, association, benefits. It's so much easier to develop strong relationships with people you respect and like and with whom you share the same values.

Am I myself with this person?

If you can't let your hair down, what's the point? Real friends accept you where you are while supporting you in becoming even better. No judgment. If you feel anxious or the need to impress, hide, or be anything other than yourself, there's a problem.

Do I want to be their friend?

This is a gut check question. You should feel drawn toward your real friends and you should stand ready to be a true friend to them. It's nice to be supported, but authentic friendships are a two-way street.

Get Moving!

Consider three friends with whom you spend the most time. Fill out the charts below, checking the statement that is true for each relationship.

Name:

☐ I am energized by this relationship.

☐ I am drained by this relationship.

☐ I can trust this person.

☐ I cannot trust this person.

☐ I like this person.

☐ I do not like this person.

☐ I can be myself with this person.

☐ I cannot be myself with this person.

☐ I want to be this person's friend.

☐ I do not want to be this person's friend.

Name:

☐ I am energized by this relationship.

☐ I can trust this person.

☐ I like this person.

☐ I can be myself with this person.

☐ I want to be this person's friend.

☐ I am drained by this relationship.

☐ I cannot trust this person.

☐ I do not like this person.

☐ I cannot be myself with this person.

☐ I do not want to be this person's friend.

Name:

☐ I am energized by this relationship.

☐ I can trust this person.

☐ I like this person.

☐ I can be myself with this person.

☐ I want to be this person's friend.

☐ I am drained by this relationship.

☐ I cannot trust this person.

☐ I do not like this person.

☐ I cannot be myself with this person.

☐ I do not want to be this person's friend.

Prayer

Lord, every day I cross paths with other people—and some of them I know You divinely orchestrated to show up in my life, whether to be a blessing to me or me to them. Give me strong discernment about my inner circle. Who are my confidants? Who has my back? Who should I let go and who should I embrace? To live the amazing life You've always imagined for me, I know I need the right people in my life—iron sharpeners, people who bring out my best, not my worst. And I need to nurture my relationships with those closest to me. Strengthen my relationship skills so that I am my authentic self. Help me forgive. Help me step into others' shoes and give me greater compassion, wisdom, and understanding. Open my eyes to habits that hold my relationships back and help me transform those habits. Amen.

Get on the Same Side

Declaration

Today, I choose to be in collaboration rather than competition.
Being on opposite sides means pushing against one another—
a guaranteed recipe for getting stuck. Even where I disagree, I
choose to at least step into the other person's shoes and make sure
they know I can see from their perspective. Getting on the same
side is a powerful tool for getting unstuck.

Key Points

- Everyone wants to feel heard, including the person who feels like your enemy right now.

- Don't just think from the other person's perspective. Verbalize your thoughts.

Sometimes, the way we get stuck is in our relationships—the ones that really matter to us. It is a scary place to want all to be well with the one you love, and yet it isn't. In the midst of frustration, knowing you're right, knowing they're wrong, and waiting for them to come to their senses and be reasonable, there is another decision you can make to get unstuck. It's very simple:

Tell them what they are saying to you makes sense.

In other words, get on the same side. Anytime you are at odds with someone, you are stuck. You are each pushing each other in the opposite direction. The only result is a stalemate. When you state sincerely, "I can see what you're saying," you cease to push away. Metaphorically, you just walked over to them, turned in the same direction, and stood side by side. Now, you are no longer the adversary. You are someone who gets it.

Once you are someone who gets it, a small opening is created for a more productive conversation where compromise can occur. This approach requires some humility. It requires you to step away from your perspective for a moment to see things through the eyes of someone else. In a positive psychology sense, you just made a deposit into the positive emotional bank account of the relationship—and specifically, this conversation. No relationship can last in a healthy, functional way when too much negativity builds up. Just as positive emotion can open your mind to make better decisions, it can open a conversation to build better outcomes.

Get Moving!

Consider for a moment a conflict or disagreement you are dealing with. Write down who it is with and what it is about.

_____

_____

_____

If you were to step away from your perspective and put yourself in the other person's shoes, what would you see that you cannot see from your side of the argument? List everything you can think of.

_____

_____

_____

What point are they trying to make that you have refused to acknowledge or see? This can be a truth that doesn't make you look good. It can be a situation that affects them negatively but doesn't really affect you. It can be a fear or anxiety they have that simply doesn't make you fearful or anxious at all. It can be an issue you wish didn't exist and you don't even know how to fix, so you'd rather avoid a discussion about it and instead want to work around it. You see where I'm going here? Can you "see what they are saying"? Right now, I want you to take a deep breath. Close your eyes and imagine the conversation from their perspective. What are they trying to say to you that you have not acknowledged or seen? Write it down here:

_____

_____

_____

Now, step back into your perspective. Take another deep breath. Seeing what you did when you stepped into their shoes, are you willing to tell them you can see it? Often, people just want to be heard. And they will fight to no end just to feel that you've heard them. So you remain stuck. Angry. Bitter. Arguing. Getting nowhere.

The truth is, you often don't even need to change your stance in order to get unstuck. You just need to see what the other is saying and acknowledge it. One surprising study at the Nottingham School of Economics showed that customers were two times more likely to forgive a company for a negative incident when the company apologized rather than giving the customer money back. In other words, the customers' frustration wasn't about money—it was about knowing the company cared and could see things from their perspective.

Prayer

Lord, help me learn to see things not just from my own perspective, but from the perspective of those You place in my path. Help me to be empathetic and compassionate rather than stubborn and self-serving. Pour out Your grace on my relationships so that they flow. Rather than getting hung up on who's right and who's wrong, help me love like You love. Help me listen and understand while still setting boundaries and doing what I know is right. Amen.

Know Your Motivation Killers

Declaration

Today, I choose to set my goals knowing exactly why I want to achieve them. I will stay motivated, not falling victim to the traps of comparing up and losing ambition. I choose to make my goals fun, finding joy in the process of achieving them.

Key Points

- Motivation is not enough. It can be easy to unwittingly zap all that motivation you've tapped into.

- Managing your thoughts is a key to managing your motivation.

Have you ever joined a gym or bought the latest exercise video only to lose motivation and quit altogether? If you're like most folks, you know what I mean. Your intentions are good, but the fiery motivation that gets you going eventually fizzles and you find yourself right back where you started—or worse. So what is the secret to lasting motivation?

Psychologists note that a key to changing your thinking is making sure your motivation is solid. Your motivation is your "why" for going after the goal—and it needs to come from the inside out. Extrinsic motivation can be enticing, but it does not hold the sort of meaning that strengthens your perseverance. For example, you could motivate yourself to lose 20 pounds so you look good for your upcoming high school reunion. But what happens after that? Intrinsic motivation is more meaningful. For example, "I finally want to experience the potential I know I am capable of," and "I want to live a long time and see my grandchildren graduate from college" are intrinsic motivations for better health. It is okay to have some extrinsic motivators, but if all of your motivation is extrinsic, you are more likely to give up when the journey to your goal becomes tough. Just as dangerous as not finding a strong enough "why" is killing your motivation through some common bad habits.

Are you guilty of one of these motivation killers?

Motivation Killer #1: Comparing "up"

When you constantly compare your body to those whom you perceive as more healthy or attractive or disciplined, you can dampen your motivation and become discouraged. It is okay to notice those around you, but do so in a balanced way. Don't just notice those who have it all together—notice the ones who are struggling too. By doing so, you realize you are not alone in your struggle. And when you compare yourself with someone who is doing better, ask empowering questions, such as, "What is she doing that helps her stay on track?" and "How does he stay away from those chocolate chip cookies?"

Solution: Instead of envy, educate yourself and learn from those who've "been there, done that."

Motivation Killer #2: Too much ambition

I know, it sounds almost un-American to tell you to curb your ambition. But too much ambition can be counterproductive. Have you ever started the New Year with a list of resolutions? It might go something like…exercise one hour per day, no soft drinks, drink eight glasses of water per day, go to bed by 9 p.m., and no midafternoon runs to the vending machine for a pack of Twinkies! By Day 3, you're failing miserably.

Solution: Choose one goal and move toward it with laser focus. After 21 days of focus, add another goal. Repeat this cycle until you reach all of your goals. Lifestyle changes happen incrementally, not overnight.

Motivation Killer #3: No fun

By going it alone or forcing yourself to do activities you truly don't like, you sap your own motivation. Team up with a buddy, take a class, or join a group activity. Make your goal ritual a social endeavor and it will be more fun. Research shows positive emotions generated by having fun actually help you persevere.

Solution: Stop thinking of exercise as a chore and find a way to make it fun.

Get Moving!

When you find yourself "comparing up" in pursuit of your goal, what positive self-talk will you use to get yourself back on track?

_____

_____

_____

You can have multiple goals, but be strategic about how much energy you allocate to each at any given time.

Considering your health, relationships, finances, career, and spiritual life, what are the top three lifestyle changes you'd like to make? (Examples: Begin each day with 15 minutes of prayer or meditation, go for a mile-long walk every day at lunch, replace the expensive latte with a glass of water.) Which habit will you focus on first? Second? Third?

_____

_____

_____

How will you make the pursuit of each of those new habits fun?

_____

_____

_____

_____

_____

_____

Prayer

Lord, I want to be the kind of person who finishes what she starts and never loses sight of the goal. Keep me from getting permanently tripped up by obstacles and pitfalls on my path. If I fail today or things don't go as planned, help me maintain an attitude of perseverance. Help me resist the temptation to compare myself constantly and only to those whom I perceive as far beyond where I am on my path. Help me set expectations that are high standards, but also realistic. And help me have fun as I move forward. Rather than seeing everything as hard work, help me find the joy. Amen.

Boost Your Brainpower

Declaration

Today, I choose to approach life as an adventure by having a growth mindset. The evidence of being fully alive is that I am growing. God created me to stretch beyond my comfort zone and try new things—experience His creation and live an amazing life.

Key Points

- Choose to see challenges as opportunities rather than setups for failure.

- A growth mindset—a willingness to try new things and put forth the effort to master them—will carry over into every area of your life.

- Embracing a life of learning can improve your brain function, stretch your potential, and add joy to your life.

How fearless are you about learning something new? A milestone birthday was the catalyst for my friend Donna to embark on an inspiring "five-year adventure plan" to learn new things, try them at destinations around the globe, and find a way to give back at each locale. Two years ago, she overcame her fear of heights by climbing Mount Kilimanjaro in Tanzania. Last year, she ran a marathon (her first) in Istanbul, Turkey. Now, she and a group of friends will go on a skydiving expedition in Florida with a decorated war veteran. The following year, it's biking along the Tour de France route. And she'll top off the five-year plan by facing her fear of deep water. "Last year, when

I went to get my scuba certification, I panicked," she says. "The only way to face my fear of deep water is to confront it." That's why she's planning a scuba diving trip.

What about you? Skydiving or trekking up Africa's highest mountain may not be your thing, but perhaps it's time to finally embark on your dream vacation or train for that upcoming 10K race. What makes some people lifelong learners, while others insist life has taught them all they need to know?

Stanford University psychologist Carol Dweck, Ph.D, has one answer. She notes that adopting a "growth mindset" rather than a "fixed mindset" leads us to see challenges as opportunities to learn as opposed to setups for failure. The result? When you have a growth mindset, you're more willing to try new things and put forth the effort required to master them. This attitude can carry over into every area of your life—for example, work, relationships, finances, even exercise habits—and can get you out of a rut time and again.

It turns out that embracing a life of learning has other major upsides: It can improve your brain function, stretch your potential, and add joy to your life. So how can you get started? With the little things: Try a new dish at your favorite restaurant or take a class on a subject you've never studied. Use these three categories as a guide to get started:

1. Explore something you didn't think you could learn. I've never been good at drawing anything more than stick figures, so when I was recently invited to take a painting class, I wasn't too hopeful. But by the end of the class, I felt like da Vinci. My painting hangs in my foyer as a reminder that I'm capable of more that I've imagined. With the right instructions and a little practice, there's a lot you can do that you've never done before.

2. Try something you've decided you're too old to learn. Think you missed the boat because you didn't master swimming as a kid? Have you always thought it would be neat to sing onstage or act in a local play? Try it for fun and your possibilities expand exponentially.

This is not about competing and performing; it's about trying something purely for pleasure. You can be awful at it, but if you like it, do it anyway! When you give yourself permission to perform badly at something that nonetheless makes you feel good while doing it, you free yourself to live more fully.

3. Stop just talking about it and do the thing you've been planning to learn someday. What have you been talking about learning to do "one day"? Conversational Italian for that dream trip to Italy? How to read a financial statement? Perhaps it's time for *someday* to become *today*. Time passes quickly. Go for it now.

Like every other part of our bodies, the brain is always changing—and yes, even as we age, it can do so for the better. Michael Merzenich, Ph.D., a pioneer in a research area called brain plasticity, says that when we learn something new, we reinvigorate our minds and improve our cognitive function. So by introducing novel activities, you're actually exercising your brain.

Get Moving!

Make it a daily goal to stretch yourself with a new project or experience or even just a different route to work. As you do, you'll build neural pathways that could literally make you younger longer. Whether you've always dreamed of playing a musical instrument or you want to dust off that long-forgotten hope of furthering your education, it's never too late to learn, and there's no ceiling on how much you can change. Author Les Brown once put it this way: "Life has no limitations except the ones you make."

What goal have you been putting off for "someday"?

_____

_____

_____

What specific steps can you take to reach that goal?

_____

_____

_____

Prayer

Lord, thank You for the miracle of my body and mind. You created me in such a way that I can grow and improve my mind simply by trying new things and committing myself to learn. Lord, help me to not get stuck in a pattern of thinking that what I know and who I am now is all there is to me. My potential is limitless. Help me approach my life as a learning adventure and open myself to all You'd like me to experience during this precious life You've given me. As I try new things, I trust You to empower my mind to expand beyond my current abilities and stretch me beyond my current capacity. Amen.

Talk About What You *Want*, Not What You Don't

Declaration

Today, I choose to speak in terms of what I want, not what I don't. When I speak in terms of what I don't want, I get mired in the negative with no focus on a solution—a sure recipe for staying stuck. When I speak of what I want, I state an intention and set a goal in motion. So today, when I find myself rehashing the things that frustrate, irritate, or scare me, I will interrupt myself mid-sentence and say, "Yeah, I get all that. But what is it that you *want*?"

Key Points

- Negative words create negative emotion. Negative emotion narrows your scope of thinking and makes it harder to move in a positive direction.

- Instead of complaining, what request could you make?

- Your words can give life to your dreams or kill them.

I t is so easy to get stuck in a rut of talking about what you don't want. The negative is more powerful than the positive, and oftentimes we unthinkingly punctuate the negative by speaking it—not just once, but repeatedly. You may find yourself explaining your problem over and over again to different friends, colleagues, or family members. You may repeat the negatives you've heard others say about a situation. Frustrated by the obstacle in front of you, you may find yourself ruminating about it—not just mentally, but verbally as well. And the more you verbalize the problem, the bigger it becomes. The bigger it becomes, the more fearful and anxious you become.

Your words have power. Are you using that power to get stuck or to become unstoppable? You are either doing one or the other.

To be clear, I do not suggest you pretend a problem does not exist by refusing to mention it. Pretending won't make it go away. But don't magnify it by overstating it or speaking about it in ways that weaken you rather than strengthen you. Instead, be very conscious of your words. Intentionally speak about obstacles or stumbling blocks in a way that empowers you to take control and improve the situation. Speak of it in ways that honor God's power to help you overcome the obstacles. Speak of it in a way that affirms the type of person you want to be in the face of a challenge. Talk about what you *want*, not what you don't.

Talking about what you want focuses your mind on the outcome you desire rather than the one you fear and dread. As a result, your energy is focused on the positive and you more naturally move toward it. Talking about what you want feels *different*. It breathes life into your situation, illuminating the positive possibilities rather than the negative ones.

Here's how you do it. Measure your words about the challenges and obstacles you face by your answers to these three questions:

- Do my words point to what I want to see happen?
- Do they acknowledge my power (however small or large) to effect change?
- Do they acknowledge God's power or what God wants for me?

Consider for a moment your relationships, finances, health, and work life. In each area, the following are examples of using your words to talk about what you want versus what you don't.

Relationship Ruts
I want peace in our relationship vs. *I'm so tired of arguing with you.*
I want to feel secure in your love for me vs. *You are so untrustworthy.*

It is important to me to feel heard vs. *You never listen.*

I love how it feels when you touch me vs. *You are never affectionate.*

Money Monsters

I want to have enough vs. *I'm tired of being broke.*

I need to increase my income vs. *They won't give me a raise.*

I am climbing out of credit card debt vs. *I am drowning in credit card debt.*

Career Cloggers

I want to find work I enjoy vs. *I hate my job.*

I am looking forward to successfully finishing this project vs. *I am dreading this project.*

I'm looking for the lesson in this situation I'm going through at work vs. *I never get the promotion.*

Health Hang-ups

I'm learning to eat healthier vs. *I can't help eating sweets/pasta/fried foods.*

I am doing my best to stay healthy vs. *I'm coming down with a cold.*

I'm experimenting with ways to enhance my appearance vs. *I hate how I look.*

Acknowledge What's Really Going On

Rather than resisting, pretending you aren't stuck, stalling, or procrastinating, say it out loud: "I'm stuck, stalling, and procrastinating! Now, what do I want?" Assuming you want to move forward, you need to redirect your thoughts and energy toward what you want. Say it out loud: "I want to take a walk to get my exercise in for the day. I want to speak up and tell that person what I need. I want to start that project and move toward my dream. I want _____." The tongue has the power of life and death (Proverbs 18:21). So stop what you are doing. Breathe. Then close your eyes and meditate on what you want. Envision yourself doing it *right now*—without fanfare, without struggle. Naturally and with ease, see yourself moving forward. The next step is simple: Move forward! Once you redirect your thoughts, it is only natural to redirect your actions.

Get Moving!

Negative words and emotions are powerful, and it's important to make sure they don't overpower the positives. In what current situations do you need to begin speaking words of life, hope, and truth?

_____

_____

_____

_____

_____

_____

Prayer

My words are powerful, God. In fact, Your Word promises the power of life and death are in my tongue. Show me where my words are hindering my progress. At times, I have used my words to contradict Your Word—doubting Your promises and believing that somehow Your promises apply to others, but not to me. Today, I ask You to remove all doubt. Make me bold in my speech. Make my words reflect an unwavering belief in Your supernatural power to move mountains and transform my life. Speak through me in a way that blesses others. Speak through me a breakthrough, a renewed life, an unstoppable spirit. Thank You for blessing me with this amazing power—my words. Now, help me stop misusing the power and start using it for the purpose for which You gave it to me—to bring life. Amen.

Begin

Declaration

Today, I choose to begin. I break free from the enemy's grip the moment I take a step forward in faith. Even if I get stuck again, I only stay stuck when I refuse to get moving. So I begin—again and again. And that is what makes me unstoppable.

Key Points

- Getting unstuck is not complicated. Take action.
- Make something small happen.
- Make something big happen.

A few years ago, my dad and I were talking about how to get up really early in the morning when you feel like hitting snooze and burying your head under the covers. He said something that always sticks with me on days when I feel like turning back over: "The key is to get your feet on the ground and keep them moving!" he advised. Simple, but true.

Moving happens with a split-second decision to sit up, swing my legs over the side of the bed, stand up, and start moving. In the heat of the moment, when my flesh says, "Just five more minutes...*pleassse!*" I have to consciously say, "No. I'm getting up now" and then follow through with my actions. Once I start moving, I keep moving! By the time I get to the bathroom and grab my toothbrush, I feel a little tinge of pride. "You did it! You didn't feel like it, but you got moving."

You have more power over your life than you tap into. That power lies in your ability to take action and make choices in a new direction. God gives you free will. He blessed you with a sound mind to make decisions. He did not give you a spirit of fear, but asks you to be bold and courageous in your steps...for He is with you. Do you hear me? *God Himself is with you.* What on earth are you waiting for?

So today, begin. Pivot. Move in the direction in which you hear the Holy Spirit leading you. It is a choice. And while sometimes the endless chatter of people and media and the doubts and fears in the back of your mind can seem overwhelming, you have the power to ignore them and do what you know it is time to do. "Faith is taking the first step even when you can't see the whole staircase," Martin Luther King, Jr. once said.

When you're trying to drown out that negative chatter, that chatter that gets you stuck, the first step can feel so huge. It can feel monumental...in your head. But really, it isn't. It is only as monumental as you make it in your mind. And the bigger you make it, the scarier it becomes. So make it small. No big deal.

First steps are simple: Make the call. Fill out the application. Initiate the conversation. Cut out the sugar. Shred the credit card. Sign up for the class. Say *I'm sorry.* Hold his hand. Buy the plane ticket. Write that letter. Open the savings account. Write down your goal.

This anonymous quote crossed my path at the grocery store the other day:

> The one thing all famous authors, world class athletes, business tycoons, singers, actors and celebrated achievers in any field have in common is that they all began their journeys when they were none of these things.

Whatever your dream, whether it is a happy marriage or a purposeful career or a healthier body or financial freedom, today can be your first step in the direction of your heart's desire. While your thoughts produce action, it is ultimately your action that creates your life. Thoughts turn you toward the right direction, but it is your faith and courage that produce action. And that is all that matters—what you do. What you do creates your reality.

What is it finally time for you to do? Begin.

Get Moving!

What is the first step you need to take as you make your dream a reality?

_____

_____

_____

What negative self-talk is keeping you from making that step?

_____

_____

_____

_____

_____

What positive thoughts will overcome the negative thinking?

_____

_____

_____

_____

_____

Prayer

Lord, I believe in a new opportunity, a dream yet to be realized or maybe even expressed. God, I'm nervous about getting started, but I know *getting unstuck starts with something simple. I must begin. I must write the first word, start the conversation, enroll in the class, have the meeting. I must simply begin. I get anxious when I think of it, God, but I know I am the only one who can take the step. No one will do it for me. But You can help me with my courage. Give me a spirit of faith to take action, to boldly forge ahead, to embrace the challenge, to live fully. Help me today to begin. Amen.*

Keep Going!

Declaration

Today, I choose to keep going in the right direction, to persevere, to persist. I am not focused on how fast I get there. I am focused on how consistently I move toward the vision God has shown me for my life. Even when I stumble, I will stumble forward.

Key Points

- Consistent action leads you to the finish line.
- Perseverance is fueled by a sense of purpose.

To begin is the beginning. After that first step, you have to manage your choices moment by moment. It may take practice. You won't do it perfectly every day. But that's okay, because each day is a new opportunity to begin again.

The moment you *do* something, you are unstuck. Even if you stumble, you still took action. So be gentle with yourself when you mess up. You're human. You're going to make mistakes. And your insistence that you are not allowed to mess up is the very reason you get stuck. If you're so careful to be perfect, you are not free. The moment you risk making a mistake is the moment you are free to give yourself wholeheartedly to trying, to living, to being unstoppable.

So just how do you keep going? Especially when you feel stuck, discouraged, or just plain scared?

Make a decision to keep going. It is within your power to choose. As my husband says often to our kids, "First you make your decisions, then your decisions make you." Perseverance doesn't just happen. You make a decision for it to happen!

Take another step. Your next step doesn't even have to be a big one. Just take one. And after you take that one, take another. Keep moving forward. What step could you take today?

Rally your support team. If you are really struggling to think the right thoughts or take the right steps, reach out to the ones who can remind you of who you are and the vision for where you are going. If you can, find someone who is moving in the same direction, tell them your goal for today, and ask them to hold you accountable. Unstoppable people don't go it alone. They reach out.

Take a walk. Physically move forward. The motion of taking literal step after step after step is a powerful metaphor for the steps you need to take forward in that situation. As you walk, imagine moving forward in the situation that feels stuck.

Get Moving!

Success is a series of good decisions. Stack them up one on top of another and you will build an incredible life. These decisions are often small ones—getting up early so you can meditate or work out, for example, or choosing the grilled fish off the menu instead of fried. Even the big decisions are carried out in small moments—for instance, saying *no* to an opportunity that will lead you away from your vision rather than closer to it.

So, will you make the call or keep procrastinating? Put on your tennis shoes to head to the gym or come up with an excuse? Will you sit down and work on that project or turn on the television? Consider these strategies to get unstuck.

4 Ways to Get Unstuck in Five Seconds

1. You know that person you're procrastinating about reaching out to? When you finish reading this, contact that person immediately. Don't wait til later. Do it *now*—while your motivation is high.

2. That thing you need to say, but can't seem to muster the courage? Remember this: All you need to do is open your mouth and say it—honestly and kindly. That's all that is standing between you and truth.

3. Ask for help from someone who is a "mover." Sometimes we just need to be around somebody with vision, someone on the move. High energy is contagious.

4. Stop thinking about your problem and think about a solution. Ask, "What's the next easiest step that will move me toward what I want?"

Feeling stuck and being stuck are not the same. Feelings are honest, but they are not necessarily the truth. I can feel like hitting the rude cashier, but that's not what I should do! Feelings come from thoughts—what you say to yourself about your dilemma. Change your thoughts and you change what you feel. Change what you feel and you change what you do.

Staying stuck is a choice. Move toward what you want. Even if it is a baby step, get moving!

What could you do to move forward?

When will you do it?

Who in your life is high energy and always moving forward, even in the face of adversity? What is the most inspiring lesson you have learned from observing them? How can you use that to inspire you right now?

Prayer

Sometimes I get tired, God. I feel like giving up. And when I feel that way, I slow down. I don't take as many steps forward. I even doubt my path. And that gets me stuck. But I know Your will for me is to be unstoppable— to keep going in the direction You lead me, even when it gets difficult, even when I cannot see how it will all come together. With Your help, I choose to keep going. I choose to persevere. Remind me to lift my eyes and look to my vision so I can remember that beautiful place I am persevering toward. Give me the strength. You will get the glory. Amen.

Lighten Up

Declaration

Today, I choose to pursue my goal unencumbered. I will not
weigh myself down with commitments, relationships,
and mindsets that do not contribute to my dream.
I will climb to the altitude to which God is calling me.

Key Points

- Don't underestimate the resources you will need to reach your goal.
- Learn to narrow your focus and set priorities in pursuit of your dream.

A young girl was taking flight lessons with the goal of becoming the youngest person to fly across the country. Her father wanted to join his daughter and the instructor on a flight. There were a couple of problems, though—rather big ones. With the fuel that was needed, the size of the airplane, and the heights to which they would be climbing along the foothills of the Rockies, adding one more passenger might just put them above the weight limits of the aircraft. And to add more reason for concern, the weather conditions were less than ideal. Despite all of this, the pilot agreed to the extra passenger and takeoff that day against his better judgment.

It was a fatal decision. As the plane attempted to climb to higher altitudes, it crashed. All three of them lost their lives that day.

It is a horribly tragic story. A girl pursuing her dream, a proud father wanting the experience of seeing her in action, and a competent pilot who didn't say *no* when he knew it was the right answer. I can't help but notice the lessons in this story that apply to each of us on the journey to getting unstuck and developing the resilience to be unstoppable:

Tell the truth. Trust your instincts.

We've talked about the importance of telling yourself the truth—and using that truth to get you unstuck by making the right decisions in the first place. When you ignore your instincts, which are a gift from God and often the voice of the Holy Spirit Himself, you step into a danger zone.

None of us does this intentionally. We don't actually believe that ignoring our instincts will lead to something as dramatic as misery or a divorce or even death. It is typically fear that causes us to ignore the instinct in favor of the less painful decision of the moment. Rather than saying *no* to someone, for example, you say *yes* even though you don't mean it. Rather than ending the dysfunctional relationship, you remain in it to avoid confrontation and "keep the peace." In reality, you have no peace at all.

When you tell the truth, you lighten your load by removing all encumbrances to getting and staying on the path of peace and grace. Once on that path, you can soar to higher heights. Sometimes that means staying on the ground until it is safe to take off or limiting who goes with you. You need to avoid carrying too heavy a load to climb to the altitude to which God is calling you. Not everyone can join you where God is taking you. If you don't accept and embrace that truth, you may limit the possibilities for your life.

A big vision requires lots of fuel.

Many capable people stall out because they underestimate how much energy they need to get to the next level. In the case of the flight that crashed, the plane required a great deal of fuel, which made the plane heavier. As a result, adding the weight of another passenger was risky. Every pound counts.

So what does that mean for your life? Consider the vision you have for your life over the next year. Being unstoppable requires you to climb to higher altitudes. You'll need fuel for that: passion, people, physical energy, spiritual fortitude, knowledge, and perhaps even financial increase. If you underestimate the significance of what it will take for you to muster all of those resources, you could find yourself in one of two predicaments.

First, you may not have enough fuel for the journey upward. Perhaps you muster the financial resources, but some of the people in your life hold you back with their negativity or lack of moral support. Or you gain new professional skills but neglect your spiritual life, and as a result are not tuned into God's guidance to help you navigate the obstacles that appear.

Second, you may have the resources, but underestimate just how much energy it takes to rally those resources. As a result, you overload your life with more activity than you can reasonably maintain and are too overloaded to climb to the next altitude in your life. You literally overwhelm yourself.

> Let us throw off everything that hinders and the sin that so easily entangles. And let us run with perseverance the race marked out for us, fixing our eyes on Jesus, the pioneer and perfecter of faith (Hebrews 12:1-2).

The higher you want to climb, the lighter your load must be.

It seems counterintuitive, but to be unstoppable you need to have less on your plate, not more. You will have to say *no* more often. You will have to narrow your focus rather than widen it. The most successful people in the world are masters of one thing, not ten. This could mean that the most important element of your next step is to start pruning.

I love what Jesus tells us in John 15:2 as He describes how to bear "much fruit" (climb to a higher altitude, be unstoppable): God "cuts off every branch in me that bears no fruit, while every branch that does bear fruit he prunes so that it will be even more fruitful."

Get Moving!

You cannot afford extra weight as you go up. Extra weight that does not help you climb is simply weight you must bear and carry. It requires energy and fuel that could be used to further your purpose, but instead it distracts you. What "weight" requires energy right now that does not further the purposes of God in your life?

_____

_____

_____

What do you need to do to remove that weight and lighten your load so you can climb to the next level God is calling you to?

_____

_____

_____

Prayer

Lord, show me what to prune from my life. How should I go about lightening my load? I want to soar to new heights and I can't do it with the weight of responsibilities You didn't ask me to take on and things that are not purposeful for me. To be honest, the idea of letting some things go scares me a bit—what if I prune the wrong thing? But God, I refuse to let fear and doubt keep me from the amazing life You have for me. I'm listening right now. I'm listening for Your voice. Speak to me, Lord. And show me how and where to lighten my load—what to say and what to do to make this process a smooth one. I want to bear much fruit. Amen.

Ask

Declaration

Today, I choose to ask for what I'm worth. I refuse to allow fear to keep me financially stuck because I don't negotiate for more. God has not given me a spirit of fear. Sometimes the key to getting unstuck lies in my willingness to speak up.

Key Points

- Women are far less likely than men to negotiate unless they are told the terms are negotiable.

- Not asking is a bad habit that you can change starting right now.

To Make More Money,
Start by Changing This One Bad Habit

don't know about you, but over the course of my career, I have certainly had occasion to realize I was underpaid for the work I was doing. In fact, the first time I was offered a job out of school, doing sports public relations, the salary they offered was abysmal. I tried to figure out how I could possibly make it on that salary, but the only way I could get by every month was for my parents to subsidize the company's pitiful offer—and I hadn't gone all the way through grad school to have my parents paying some of my bills. It didn't occur to me to tell the company I'd come to work for them if they paid me more money, so I simply turned the job down. I shake my head just thinking about it.

If you've heard the frenzy of discussion about women getting equal pay for equal work, you've heard the statistic that women earn on average about 77 cents for every dollar a man makes. It is a disturbing trend indeed.

Under-earning is the condition of being paid less money for doing *exactly* the same work someone else is doing. It is often presented as purely an issue of sexism. But the issue is deeper than that. It is something I talk about briefly in *Happy Women Live Better* in the chapter on the happiness trigger I call "financial savvy." The issue is this: Too often, women don't ask for more money. Men do.

Consider this excerpt from the book:

> One of the rarely discussed reasons for the persistent gap between men's and women's pay could be the fact that men are much more likely than women to negotiate. In a study of almost 2,500 job seekers by the National Bureau of Economic Research, it was found that when an employer does not explicitly state that wages are negotiable, men are more likely than women to negotiate...So the pay gap between men and women is significantly more pronounced in jobs where wage negotiation is ambiguous.

There are certainly gender disparities that are rooted in institutionalized prejudice and the devaluing of jobs that are traditionally held by women. However, successful women think differently. They don't just focus on problems beyond their immediate control and see themselves as victims. They ask, "What do I have control over that can positively impact my situation?" You control whether or not you negotiate. You control whether or not you speak up and ask for more. You control whether you settle for less than you deserve or have the courage to pursue opportunities that will boost your income. Not asking is a bad habit—one you can change right away.

Don't sell yourself short. Raise your standards and expect more.

**You don't get what you deserve; you get what you accept.
Believe in your worth and ask for more.**

I'll never forget the moment a business owner who'd spent years booking speakers told me I could charge double what I was asking. I looked at him, stunned. "You're already there," he said. "You just need to ask for more." The idea of asking for twice what I'd been charging felt both exciting and scary. *Was he sure?* But I knew the answer. He'd booked hundreds of speakers. He knew what he was talking about. And I'd seen the speakers who were making more. They weren't better speakers than I, just better negotiators!

I went away from the meeting and halfway took his advice. Not yet bold enough to ask for double, the next time a major company called, I quoted a rate that was 50 percent higher than my previous fee. The decision maker didn't bat an eye. Just like that, a 50 percent increase for doing exactly the same work!

A year later, I made the leap he suggested and doubled my fee. Clients didn't flee. In fact, I got more speaking opportunities than ever. Raising my fee also led me to upgrade my marketing and work harder to provide even more value. It was a turning point for me personally, professionally, and financially. Today, perhaps you are reading these words because it is time for a turning point of your own.

Get Moving!

In what way is it time to ask for more?

_____

_____

_____

What are you afraid will happen if you do?

_____

_____

_____

Despite any fear, will you just go ahead and ask anyway?

Prayer

What do I need to ask for today, God? I'm asking You because sometimes I am so hesitant to ask that I no longer recognize what I need. So open my eyes to the ways in which I allow fear or lack of negotiation skills to keep me from asking for help or asking for what I deserve. It is possible that the gap between where I am and where I want to be lies in a ten-second question! Show me the question. Show me who to ask. Help me develop the courage and boldness to simply ask. Give me the heart not to be dissuaded, embarrassed, or hurt if the answer is no or not now. Will You give me the wisdom and courage I need to ask the right question of the right person to move me forward today? I'm so grateful for Your guidance. Amen.

Get Mad, Cry It Out

Declaration

Today, I choose to let myself be human and feel what I feel. It is healthy to cry, to feel angry, and to experience my emotions rather than stuff them down. I will find healthy ways to express my negative emotions and allow them to wash through me. When I do, I unclog my stopped-up emotional drain so that love, faith, and courage can once again flow through me unhindered by bitterness, negativity, or anger.

Key Points

- When you work through your feelings, you clear the way to move forward.

- Negative emotions are normal, but they are not an excuse to hurt others.

Crying moments are pivotal moments. Unable to hold the well of emotion in any longer, the well runs over and the tears spill out from within—literally. It can be a scary thing, crying—especially when there is nothing in the moment you can do to change your circumstances. But it is the act itself of crying that gives you what you so desperately need: release. Crying is honest. It is raw. It is your truth. And the pure truth of your tears can clear away the stuff that gets in the way of surrender.

It is a myth that crying is a sign of weakness. Your willingness to feel your feelings is a sign of true strength. In fact, what has you stuck may be the unwillingness to allow those feelings that have been trying so hard to bubble up to the surface. And as they attempt to come up and keep getting pushed down, they create an emotional blockage that gets you stuck and unable to freely move forward.

I recall a friend telling me of a change she'd seen in me after I got unstuck. "You seem so much more relaxed now. It used to seem like you were just holding it together." I was shocked. I never thought anyone could see my stress or anxiety. But she had seen it as clear as day. I'd never thought of it that way, but she was right. I had been "holding it together." I was holding a lot together. I had been miserable and didn't want anyone to know. I was afraid of being judged if my life didn't appear perfect. Holding it together was about holding in the truth—keeping the tears inside.

Our most pivotal moments often come after the biggest moments of frustration and emotional turmoil.

Get Moving!

Describe a situation in which you tried to hide your true emotions.

_____

_____

_____

_____

_____

Describe a situation in which you allowed yourself to show what you were really feeling.

_____

_____

_____

_____

_____

How were the outcomes of the two situations different?

_____

_____

_____

Prayer

Lord, help me healthfully release any emotions that block me from moving forward. Help me process my frustrations and hurts rather than stuffing them down. Restore my soul, Lord. Renew my spirit. Give me the bravery to admit where I need healing and the humility to allow myself permission to feel what I feel. Then, once I release those emotions, put me back together again. Let Your Spirit and wisdom flow through me. Amen.

Stop Staring at the Closed Door

Declaration

Today, I choose to let go of the past and courageously face forward. When I stare at the closed doors, I miss the open doors and cracked windows that lie before me.

Key Points

- Holding on to the past weighs you down and creates baggage that is too heavy to carry into the future God imagines for you.

- Trust God to cause all things to work together for good.

wrote my book *Where Will You Go from Here?* after digging myself out of a big ditch. I had started my life over and I identified Five Commitments we must make if we are going to bounce back and start life again:

1. I will not feel sorry for myself.

2. I will not stare at the closed door.

3. I will dig deep to unearth all the courage I need.

4. I will direct my thoughts. My thoughts will not direct me.

5. I will choose to believe all things work together for good.

Over the years, the commitment that has resonated most with readers was, "I will not stare at the closed door." One of the most common ways we can get stuck is by dwelling too long on what used to be.

We stare longingly at what life was and refuse to embrace what life is. When faced with a new normal, whether becoming single after years of marriage, getting laid off, or any circumstance we'd preferred not to have, it is impossible to thrive if you insist life must be what it once was in order for you to be happy and live successfully.

Get Moving!

Is there a past situation you need to let go of in order to move into the future God has for you? What are you afraid will happen if you let go of it?

_____

_____

_____

What do you hope will happen if you open yourself up to a new but uncertain future?

_____

_____

_____

Prayer

Lord, although some doors have closed, help me face the future with a vision of better things to come. When I get stuck thinking about what "should have been" or "would have been," please remind me of what "could be" if I embrace the future with faith. Today, I choose to trust that if the door is closed, it is not one You want me to walk through—at least not right now. I choose to believe that a better door can open eventually, but I will not see it if I'm staring at the closed one behind me. Help me bounce back from my disappointment. Strengthen me for the journey ahead. Amen.

Be Gentle with Yourself

Declaration

Today, I choose to be gentle with myself—to give myself breaks
when I am tired, ask for help when I need it, and learn from
my mistakes rather than beat myself up for them.
When I start down the harsh road of criticism, shame,
or unreasonable deadlines, I will stop, breathe, and pray.

Key Points

- Goal fatigue is real. Keep your energy replenished or you will burn out.

- Being your own worst critic does not make you unstoppable. It makes you unreasonable.

- Self-forgiveness frees you from the enemy's grip of guilt and shame.

A high school freshman soccer team had a run of horrible luck. They got a new coach who had been a terrific college player but was a not-so-terrific coach. They lost every single game that season. One parent thought the way to motivate his son to play better and help the team was to punish him every time they lost. In fact, the poor kid got grounded after every loss. I would argue the father's approach was abusive. At the very least, it was counterproductive. As the season went on, his son's motivation plummeted. Soon, he was ready for the season to be over. The sport he once loved he now dreaded.

Not only that, he didn't want to try any other sports because they now seemed nothing more than a setup for failure and punishment.

What Good Is Beating Yourself Up?

If every time we don't reach the goal—or don't reach it in perfect fashion—we get beat up and punished, eventually our motivation to keep trying can begin to diminish. But unlike the story above, we're the ones beating ourselves up. Our expectations of what we should achieve and how we should achieve it can be unreasonably high. If you give yourself no margin for error, when you veer off course you can focus so much on your mistake that you lose perspective. If you expect perfection, you are guaranteed to fall short at some point.

God gives us grace. He looks at our hearts and our efforts. He wants us to learn and grow from our mistakes, not ruminate on them. When you ruminate or repeatedly mull over what went wrong, you get stuck. When you beat yourself up, what are you actually accomplishing? What do you get out of it? We do everything for a payoff. Getting unstuck from bad habits is largely about understanding the payoff you get from continuing in that pattern of behavior. Here are a few common "benefits" of beating yourself up.

You get to be the victim. As a victim, you get the attention—and this can divert eyes from the real issue. You can get sympathy from others and sometimes even manipulate them in some way. If you are the victim, you may be able to escape harsh judgment or consequences. You may be looking for compassion that is lacking from others, and victimhood is a way to get it. Caring people find it difficult to ignore the plight of others. Ultimately, the greatest judgment you may seek to escape is God's. Ouch. If you are a victim, maybe God won't blame you for not being obedient. After all, your fear/anxiety/stress was so intense. The situation was so unfair. The people were so difficult. How could you be expected to overcome such odds?

It creates a distraction from taking action. Sometimes beating yourself up is just another excuse to procrastinate. Instead of taking action, you analyze, you cry, you get angry, and you blame yourself for not being able to do more.

Negative reinforcement and motivation. The prospect of avoiding pain (beating yourself up) can be considered a motivator. Most of what we do is either to avoid pain or embrace joy. The soccer player's parent, for example, attempted to motivate his son with the threat of pain, hoping the son would be so motivated to avoid the pain that he would somehow save the team from defeat. You can do the same to yourself, but at some point, you want to be intrinsically motivated— to be driven by an innate desire to live fully, do your best, and experience the reward of living your life on purpose. When you finally, truly become unstoppable, it will be out of your desire to live a faith-filled life that is whole, purposeful, and pleasing to God.

"Paying" for your sins. This boils down to forgiveness. Our sins are paid for. But the person who beats herself up rarely forgives her own sins. The line of thinking is that being hard on oneself is the way to pay for mistakes.

Lessen the sting of real consequences. If you beat yourself up more than others beat you up, then their judgment perhaps will not feel like such a rebuke. In other words, beating yourself up can serve as a coping mechanism that protects you from hurt and rejection.

So there is payoff for beating yourself up. Which of the above benefits most resonate as the reason you beat yourself up when you make mistakes on your way to a goal?

Is Your Ambition Wearing You Out?

What is the balance between ambition and contentment? Does it exist and do you need it? The answer is yes. The balance between ambition and contentment lies in your ability to move at a divine pace— to be completely in tune with God's requirement of rest, reward, and replenishment. What tends to throw us off track is that we forego rest, focus on the wrong types of rewards, and fail to replenish the energy required to persevere in the face of obstacles and challenges.

First, let's talk about rest. God clearly created us to rest. Even He rested on the seventh day. Somehow, we've decided we don't need much rest. We can just keep going and going and expect there are no consequences to delaying rest. Researchers have identified something called "goal fatigue" that backs up the godly concept of rest. Goal fatigue theory says that a certain amount of energy is required to reach a goal. In your journey to the goal, your well of energy becomes depleted. That well must be replenished in order for you to have the same reservoir of energy for your next goal. Otherwise, the personal resources available to reach the next milestone are diminished. If this cycle continues without rest and replenishment, eventually your well of energy will run completely dry. Call it goal fatigue. Call it burnout. Call it whatever you like, but take note. You need rest. There is freedom in rest. If you cannot take a break or a day off, you are not free.

Second, if the rewards you are after are unevenly extrinsic—focused on external or materialistic gain—you may eventually lose motivation. Additionally, driving yourself without rewarding yourself for making progress can stunt motivation.

Third, give yourself the time to replenish. Replenishing is about more than rest. It is about restoration. As you forge ahead, there will be bumps in the road that will ding your armor, damaging your confidence and even your sense of self. In these instances, you don't just need rest. You need God to restore your soul.

There may be lessons that need to be learned. And you can't get unstuck and be unstoppable until you do. It is essential that you be gentle enough with yourself to recognize when you need to stop, tune in to God, and give Him the time and opportunity to do a work of restoration. For example, in a relationship that has endured hurts and anger, you need more than a romantic getaway to generate restoration. In your finances, you may need more than just a good raise to fix your challenges. A raise won't remove that foreclosure from your credit report. That will take time. When you have surgery to fix a broken bone, you may need more than rest. You'll also need rehab to restore your body to full ability.

One of the many reasons we get stuck is that we allow pure ambition, or (as the Bible calls it) "selfish ambition," to drive us to relentlessly pursue goals without the benefit of rest, reward, and restoration as we need it. God is not a harsh taskmaster. He says His yoke is easy and His burden is light. He expects us to live a life of faith, but that life of faith must be pursued as Jesus pursued His own life of faith—at a divine pace. God is gentle. We should be just as gentle with ourselves.

Get Moving!

Be gentle with yourself. If you gave yourself rest, reward, and restoration, what would you do differently? Do that. If you can't think of anything, try these ideas:

- Take a break.
- Take a vacation.
- Pull back on some obligations and press in to God to deal with hurts and other issues that you need to be restored from.
- Reward yourself for your efforts! Acknowledge your milestones. Slow down and enjoy this journey.

Prayer

God, help me be gentle with myself. Sometimes I don't give myself a break at all. It feels as though I am driving so hard to reach a destination, but even as I reach milestones, I don't celebrate! You have brought me such a long way. Help me not take my progress for granted. Help me embrace a divine pace that reflects Your wisdom. I want to walk perfectly in Your will. Only then will I be unstoppable. Amen.

Let It Get Messy

Declaration

Today I choose to embrace the fact that sometimes chaos is the first step to clarity. Before I can organize the "closet" of my life, I have to see what is in there. That often means pulling it all out and letting it get messy so I can see what should stay, what must go, and what missing pieces I need to find.

Key Points

- Progress is a process.
- Seeing the whole picture is essential for putting things into perspective.

Have you ever finally started cleaning out a closet and created a bigger mess than if you'd left everything in there? But then it is too late to just stuff it all back in. No, you are in too deep for that. The only way to get out of the mess is to just finish what you started.

It always takes longer than you thought. You find stuff you didn't expect to find—maybe even a few long-lost treasures. "That's where my ring went!" "Look, a $20 bill!" The work you thought would take an hour ends up taking all day—or maybe all weekend. But when you are done, the feeling of triumph is so gratifying. You are energized. You know where things are. You perhaps arranged them in a way that allows you to be more productive and efficient. Rather than dreading opening the closet and looking hopelessly for your shoes, you actually open the door and stand there for a moment, admiring what you've created.

The same holds true when we are ready to get unstuck. Your situation can look like that chaotic closet. When you start taking steps forward, it gets messy. There's more to it than you thought. It will take longer than you planned and be more complicated than you expected. But if you just keep pushing through, there is a turning point when the light faintly emerges at the end of the tunnel.

And there is something else that happens when we dive into the chaotic mess. The process forces us to decide what to keep and what to get rid of. But it also illuminates one more category: what to add. It is hard to know what's missing when you aren't even clear what's present. As you seek clarity and direction in your own life, this revelation is an important one.

In our real lives, we are often afraid of messy. We are told to "hold it together." So it can be tempting to hold together a mess rather than letting it fall apart so you can reconstruct something worthy of God's intentions for you. That conversation that needs to be had might get messy, but if based in truth, it will shift the relationship to a more authentic place. If you start moving in a new direction from that career that, if you are totally honest, is not working for you, it will get messy for a while. You might have to straddle two careers simultaneously. You might have your day job and your side gig. You might go to work *and* go to school and have to be careful about who knows of your plans lest it negatively affect the job that pays the bills right now.

Between stuck and unstoppable, it can get messy. When you unpack that closet, you may realize that straightening your path means dealing with more obstacles than you expected. Be prepared for it. Progress is a process, not an event. Dig your heels in and stick with it.

Get Moving!

Break your procrastination-prone projects into bite-sized goals that allow you to feel you are making progress.

Consider a task which feels overwhelming. How could you break the job into manageable pieces? What step will you take today? By which date will you cross this item off your to-do list?

_____

_____

_____

_____

How will you celebrate or acknowledge each step along the way to your goal?

_____

_____

Prayer

God, I feel overwhelmed by the chaos of the situation I'm dealing with. I don't which way to go or when to make a move. I don't know where to start. I feel so out of control, and I'm not used to that. As a result, I feel paralyzed to move in any direction. But I also believe that clarity can come out of chaos, so help me relax in the midst of what feels like a mess. Help me find the message in this mess. Speak that message so loud to me, Lord, that it is impossible for me to miss it. Out of chaos, bring me clarity. Amen.

Find an App

Declaration

Today, I choose to use technology to get me unstuck.
Whether it's an app that helps me track my eating habits, a
reminder on my calendar, or software that makes something
complicated suddenly easier, I will find a practical tool
that makes reaching my goal just a bit easier.

Key Points

- You don't have to go it alone. Explore tools that will assist you in pursuit of your goal.

- Sometimes, the best technique for getting unstuck is to notice what got you unstuck somewhere else in your life.

I should have known it would happen. I almost got stuck when it was time to write the book on getting unstuck. Overanalyzing. Overthinking. Then, sitting in a hotel room preparing to speak at a conference in the morning on the subject of getting unstuck and being unstoppable, I happened upon a simple tool.

I'd started using a fitness app on my phone and was amazed at how much more aware and intentional I'd become about eating and exercising. The app allowed me to set specific goals and log my meals and exercise—even four-minute stints of calisthenics or six-minute walks through the airport dragging my luggage behind me. At the end of each day, I could see how well I did at nutrition, calories, fat, and more. Suddenly, I found myself squeezing in workouts and trading my juice for water. My husband and I were even "friends" on the app so we could see how the other was doing. I'd fallen off my exercise routine and now suddenly, I was back on track. I'd gotten a little too buddy-buddy with pasta and alfredo sauce, and now here I was happily devouring spinach and avocado salads. How could a simple little app get me unstuck? That was when it occurred to me, "Gee, I wish they had an app for writers!"

Hmm. Maybe they do. Sure, enough. I found one. I can log how long I write, how much I write, and how much progress I've made toward my goal.

Get Moving!

Sometimes, the best technique for getting unstuck is to notice what got you unstuck somewhere else in your life. Consider an area in which you were once stuck but are now unstoppable. You found a strategy that works and were able to change your habits. What empowered you to get moving?

_____

_____

_____

Now, how could you apply a similar technique to an area where you just can't seem to get going?

_____

_____

_____

Prayer

Lord, You've helped me get unstuck before. Now, I ask You to show me how to learn from my past successes. Show me the key lessons that empowered me to break through in a previous area of my life. Help me use those lessons as I seek to move forward in new ways. Help me tap into creativity and wisdom to see clearly and give me the confidence to break through today. Amen.

Want Less, Get More

Declaration

Today, I choose to have *enough*. I will not chase after a vision that is not authentic to me and will not bring me lasting happiness. I choose to see the blessing in what I have instead of constantly struggling to attain more.

Key Points

- Hesitation in reaching a goal may be an indication that the goal is not authentic for you.

- As you adapt to continually improving circumstances, you can start to believe that you can never have *enough*.

Have you ever wanted something, but when you finally got the opportunity, you dragged your feet? Maybe you become enamored with the idea of the goal, but not the process of getting to it. You picture yourself at the finish line—you look good, your surroundings are just right. Surely, this is where you are meant to be.

But what if it isn't? What if the goal is more of a fantasy you've conjured about the way your life should look? But truth be told, you don't want to do what is necessary to get it to look that way. Maybe real life isn't as fulfilling as your fantasy alludes. Maybe it represents what others expect of you more than what you expect of yourself. Or maybe, just maybe, if you get really honest, *you don't really care that much about reaching the goal.* You can take it or leave it. You'd prefer to take it because it would be nice. But "nice" isn't enough for the sacrifice of time, energy, and even relationships that will be required in exchange. This is what you know in your spirit, but are afraid to hear and acknowledge.

As you mature, you become more selective about what gets your time and energy. It can be easy not to notice how you're filled beyond capacity until you try to keep doing things at the pace you did before you got the higher-paying (translation: more responsibility, time, and consequences) position or the new marriage or the children or the parents you are taking care of or perhaps even the divorce that has left you the single head of household. It is easy not to notice until one day, you find yourself simply unable to keep up.

Here's the thing. You can't do everything, but you can certainly convince yourself that you can. Somewhere along the way, you can get stuck constantly wanting more—believing that what you have isn't enough and therefore, continually taking on more. When do you have enough? When do you win? Or is the quest for an amazing life/career/partner/body a never-ending one?

If the quest is futile, then your efforts are futile. And surely, that is not God's plan for you. There must be a point at which you can relax, enjoy where you are, and even stop climbing for a while and allow yourself to just *be*. This can be a hard concept for those of us who have bought into our culture of constant striving. It requires a redirection of the definition of success.

Herein lies the problem. We tend to believe we know what will make us happy. In *Successful Women Think Differently,* I dedicated an entire chapter to the idea of stepping off the "hedonic treadmill." Research shows human beings are pretty poor predictors of what makes us happy. We are sure we know, so we chase after our dream. Then we get it. We love it. We are happy. For a while.

Then we get used to it. Our happiness drops back to where it was before we got what we just *knew* we had to have. Now, we insist if we could just get that *next* thing, *then* we would be happy. And the cycle starts all over again. We adapt to continually improving circumstances. This is called hedonic adaptation.

You can step off the hedonic treadmill and counter hedonic adaptation by getting clear that wanting and attaining more is not the path to authentic happiness. This is particularly relevant when you find yourself continually achieving, yet never feeling satisfied. If it is always about the next big thing, beware. You may eventually find that even the things that used to excite you no longer compel you to move forward. You are confused about why you feel stuck. You should be excited. But perhaps the thrill you once got from the activity has worn off. You must decide when enough is enough. Pat yourself on the back. Give yourself permission to drop goals that are no longer purposeful, no longer stretch you, and that you are no longer anointed to do.

Be very intentional about wanting less. I'm not saying "want nothing," but make sure your "wants" reflect only what needs to be on your plate right now. This means you might start taking longer to make commitments or say yes to requests. You stop telling yourself that the attainment of a certain station in life is what will satisfy you. You have a talk with God *and* follow what you hear. It will take courage. It may mean a major shift in how you live or work. But it will also free you to step into the amazing life God has for you

When you stop believing you need more, you begin wanting less. The less you want, the happier you are. Which takes us back to the original question: Have you ever been in a place where you thought you wanted to do something, but when you finally got the opportunity, you dragged your feet? Think of it not as an opportunity to beat yourself up and force yourself forward, but to step back and reflect on your hesitation. What does that hesitation tell you? And what do you need to do differently as a result? Hesitation can be a tremendous spiritual gift. Pay attention.

Get Moving!

Have you ever stopped short of reaching for a goal? What made you hold back?

_____

_____

_____

_____

_____

Prayer

Lord, You have blessed me abundantly. Even if You blessed me no further, I am grateful for the grace and mercy You've shown me, for the love of friends and family, and for the opportunities I have been given. It is so easy to get stuck in a pattern of always wanting more and expecting more without appreciating what is already present in my life. It can be tempting to believe that being unstoppable is about stacking up more accomplishments, but Lord, today I ask You to help me stack up more contentment. Help me find peace and rest in the abundance that already exists in my life rather than getting caught up in the constant messages that bombard me, screaming, "You need more. You're not there yet. You're not enough yet." Empower me to do my best and pursue my mission while wanting only what You want for me—and finding deep joy in the process. Amen.

Build Some Momentum

Declaration

I choose to take steps forward every single day.
They don't have to be big steps. They just have to move me closer
to my goal. While big steps get me excited, small steps
get me moving—right away. When I focus on small steps,
I build momentum that snowballs into big strides.

Key Points

- It is easy to focus on big steps, but small steps with consistency transform your habits, sustain your energy, and get you to your destination.

- Become a master at breaking big steps into smaller ones.

A large part of becoming unstoppable is about building momentum. Getting unstuck happens the moment you take steps forward, but you remain unstuck when you *keep* moving forward. That's the part that trips most people up. They take a few steps, but at some point they stop. The critical key is to figure how *not to stop*.

It sounds so elementary. That's because it is. But even though it sounds easy, you've probably noticed the easier thing is to just stay right where you are—staring up at the big mountain that is your dream, your goal, your destiny.

Picture the scene with me for a moment. There's little ol' you, standing at the bottom of a mountain staring up to the top. It is 10,000 feet high and you don't even stand at 10 feet! As you look up, the idea that you could conquer the mountain seems irrational. It looks big…really big. You look so tiny and it looks so enormous. At moments, you feel as if you have no idea where to start.

This is where things get foggy. Overwhelm sets in. Fear. Who do you think you are? What makes you think you can conquer such a big mountain? How on earth will you do it? These are great questions to answer, and in fact, play the "what if?" game with.

Answering the last question is quite simple. I call it "chunking it," and there are four simple rules to help you do it. Chunking simply means you break down your steps to a manageable, bite-sized piece you can chew on *today*. A "chunk" is not something that takes days or weeks to accomplish. A chunk is a piece you can handle right now. This idea works because no matter what you need to accomplish, it can only be done one action at a time. The small actions are not overwhelming. It is the string of small actions that become monumental when they are not reduced to something less consuming. Here's how to chunk:

1. Make a list of absolutely everything you can think of that needs to happen in order to get to your destination. This list doesn't have to be in order. It just needs to be comprehensive. Get everything on paper so you can see it.

2. Drill down to the smallest step. The to-do's on your list are not feasible until they become something you can accomplish today—like in five minutes, or at the most, a few hours. Now in some instances you will need to repeat the steps consistently, but to be clear, a project that takes two months is too big of a project. Break it into small steps that chip away at your goal.

3. Choose the next feasible thing you can do to move forward. Do it! Once you have drilled down to small steps, you have a variety of actions to choose from. The key is to build momentum. Sometimes, it doesn't even matter in what order you take actions. It just matters that you take action.

4. Keep chipping away at your list of steps. Consistency

is what makes you unstoppable. Even if you take a few steps back, make a mistake, or do something wrong, keep chipping away at your small action steps. It is like strength training for your life. You build endurance and focus and ultimately the life God created you to have.

Jayna was at a stalemate in the parenting of her son. She and her husband had recently traveled with their child to a family holiday where the ridiculousness of their child's behavior caused Jayna to feel embarrassed and out of control with her parenting. She could hide the problems when it was just the three of them at home, but when surrounded by family members and friends, her son's behavior became glaringly problematic—especially when her sister's children behaved so well. Jayna knew she had been too lenient, and her husband traveled five days a week and was of very little help. When he came home on weekends, he was both frustrated by his son's antics and too exhausted to do much about them.

Because the task of changing her child's behavior felt so overwhelming, I asked Jayna to begin "chunking." She came up with a list:

- Talk to her sister about how she parents.
- Buy some books on parenting.
- Research extracurricular activities that could positively redirect his behavior.
- Choose an extracurricular activity based on the research.
- Pray about the problems.
- Forgive herself for her parental "shortcomings."
- Make a list of friends who could be a support system and sounding board.
- Decide what kind of support she needs from friends.
- Reach out to friends to seek support.
- Find a Christian marriage and family therapist or parenting coach.

- Talk to the therapist or coach about her stress and improving family dynamics.

- Establish new rules or approaches to use with her son.

This is a list Jayna came up with in under five minutes! She later added more to the list, but these steps were small enough that she could begin to act immediately on them. You must create small enough steps that moving forward feels simple and inspiring.

Get Moving!

What would it look like to "chunk" your own list right now? Identify your mountain and chunk your steps by making an initial list of actionable steps you can take in a matter of minutes and no more than a day:

_____

_____

_____

_____

_____

_____

Prayer

Lord, show me the actionable steps You want me to take. Help me get clear about what they are and to be intentional about keeping the list in front of me so that I can build momentum over time. I trust that You will move me forward if I listen for Your voice. Show me the vision. Make it plain! Amen.

Own Your Happiness

Declaration

Today, I choose to find joy in my everyday circumstances. I will adopt a positive outlook no matter what life throws at me. I will not let any person or situation dictate my attitude or response, but will take responsibility for my own happiness.

Key Points

- You are in charge of your own happiness. Take responsibility for your choices and your life's path.

- If you choose a bad attitude, own up to it. Your happiness is not defined by your circumstances.

- When frustration impacts your attitude, you are more likely to make choices you'll later regret.

Most people are about as happy as they make up their minds to be," Abraham Lincoln once remarked. And he was right. Another way you can get stuck is by believing your happiness lies in the hands of people, circumstances, and even God Himself. But God can't force you to be grateful, serve others, live your purpose, or be happy. Your circumstances can change, but if you cannot be content with what you have now, you'll soon find a reason to be unhappy with your new circumstances.

How do you own your happiness?

Take responsibility for your life's path.

"If you're not living your vision, you're probably living someone else's," Pastor Dennis Rouse once said. While it is certainly good to be a part of something bigger than yourself—a team, a partnership, an organization—you need to be clear about the divine vision for *your* life. You need a clear path. Pray about it. Plan it. Proceed. Take responsibility for the direction of your life rather than simply doing what others want or not having a clear direction at all.

Take responsibility for your choices.

When the choices are great, take responsibility. Notice how your choices have led to the outcome. This is empowering because it helps you see that more good choices can lead to more good outcomes. Likewise, when you make bad choices, own them. Ask God's forgiveness. Ask God for the lesson, too. If you hurt someone in the process, apologize. If you hurt yourself in the process, forgive yourself.

Choose your attitude.

Yes, some people have a sunny disposition, but for the most part happiness is a *choice*. Almost half of your happiness (according to researchers the number is 40 percent, to be exact) is made up of the intentional choices you make every day—to be grateful, connect with people, or make somebody smile, for example. If you choose a bad attitude, own up to it. Bad moods happen, so have a plan to deal with them. Tell the people around you that you need time to regroup, acknowledge that you realize your attitude is not the best, and don't say much since you know what you say will likely come out the wrong way. Then get unstuck with a decision: Choose a better attitude. You're the only one who can make that choice for you.

Be intentional about who you spend time with.

Happiness is contagious. Even the research bears this out. Having at least one happy person in your circle increases your chances of being happy by 15 percent. Even a $10,000 raise only boosts your happiness by 10 percent. Likewise, miserable, pessimistic people are contagious, too. So if you want to be happy, choose your cast and crew wisely.

Stop expecting people to change who won't.

Ask for change, but don't depend on change. Pray for them, but keep moving forward with God's plans for your life. Your job is to stay focused on your vision and invite them to be a part of it.

Get Moving!

The last time you climbed your way out of a bad mood, what actions did you take to change your attitude?

_____

_____

_____

_____

_____

How have you seen your attitude affect the outcome of a situation?

_____

_____

_____

_____

Prayer

God, shine a light on the self-sabotage I create when I say things that speak death into my dreams and shatter my hopes. When I am tempted to say, "I can't," prompt me to say instead, "I can do all things through Christ who strengthens me." When I am tempted to use my words to beat myself up, inspire me instead to acknowledge my efforts and be gentle with myself. When I am tempted to use my words to rehash my problems, remind me to use my words to brainstorm solutions. Transform my words to reflect what You say about me—that I am fearfully and wonderfully made, that I am loved, that I am bold and courageous and strong, that You have a purpose for my life. Amen.

Do Your Own "Year in Review"

Declaration

Today, I choose to reflect on the biggest lessons life has offered me
over the last year. By being intentionally self-reflective,
I mark my lessons as a milestone and ask myself,
"Where can I apply these lessons right now?"

Key Points

- A self-reflective recap helps you see how much richer you
  are in wisdom than you were this time last year.

- Notice how your progress empowers you to realize how far
  you've already come—and how unstoppable you really are.

Every year, we are bombarded with "Year in Review" headlines.
The best dressed, the top songs, and most fascinating people of
the year. But I like to do my own "Year in Review," and it doesn't
have to be at the end of December.

Look back over the last 12 months and do a self-reflective recap that
helps you see how much richer you are in wisdom than you were this
time last year. Noticing your progress empowers you to realize how far
you've come—and how unstoppable you really are. "Blessed are those
who find wisdom, those who gain understanding, for she is more prof-
itable than silver and yields better returns than gold," says Proverbs
3:13-14. As time passes, you ought to find yourself continually richer.
Whether you view the experiences of the last year as good or bad, each
one offers an opportunity to become richer in wisdom and better prepared to live wisely and be resilient.

Here's what I learned over the past year. How about you?

Patience is relaxing. From the moment I entered kindergarten a year early, I've always been on the fast track. I put a high value on doing things fast. Whether it was squeezing too much into my schedule, finishing college in three years, or exceeding the speed limit, I always rushed toward a proverbial finish line. But this year, I sensed a major shift in my spirit. I learned this year that patience means a more relaxing approach to life. Whether you are trying to decide if a relationship is right for you or if it's time to change careers, the answers don't always come quickly. Be okay with that. Trust that divine timing is often not your timing—but it is perfect timing. Rather than rushing, rest. Enjoy the journey.

Love is action. True love is action—it's what you do because you decide to love a person unconditionally. It is not always easy, but it allows you the stability of knowing where you stand independent of what the other person does. That's how God loves us. In spite of our faults and mistakes, selfishness or sin, He loves us. Nothing we do can change that. Can you love like that?

The key to success is sticking with it. This year was our business's best year yet. In nearly 12 years of business, there have been times when I was tempted to give up, get a job, or doubt my path. But I never acted on those temptations. Deep down, I know I am called to this work. It is a part of who I am. So whatever it has required, I've stuck with it. Thank goodness. I can't imagine doing anything other than inspiring you to get unstuck, be unstoppable, and live the fulfilling life you were called to live.

Happiness is embracing what is and saying, "Thank You for this life of mine." I know you have goals. In fact, as humans we can't be happy without goals. We need something to aim for. But while we are aiming, during that period in the meantime when we haven't quite obtained what we want—there is a lesson being offered. It is a gift. It is the chance to learn to be happy *while*, not just happy *when*. Happy while you wait, not just happy when you arrive. When you master that, you discover the key to contentment. Embrace what is and find reasons to be grateful right where you are.

Get Moving!

Reflect on the wisdom you've gained over the last 12 months. What have you learned?

_____

_____

_____

_____

_____

_____

_____

How will you apply those lessons in the next 12 months?

_____

_____

_____

_____

_____

_____

Prayer

It is so easy to notice what I haven't done, but God, help me see and celebrate what I have done! I know You celebrate each step I take. When I see my progress, it gives me hope and energy to keep moving forward. So help *me acknowledge my milestones. They are reason to praise You and reason to affirm my efforts. Today, as I notice my progress, help me see the lesson I can glean from my journey. What is the most important lesson You want me to learn from the last year? What is the most significant milestone? What required my faith in action? What do You most want from me in the year that lies ahead? Reveal the answer to me, God. I want to squeeze every bit of wisdom from my journey. Amen.*

Be God's Ambassador

Declaration

Today, I choose to glorify God through
the example I set for others. I will step out in faith to be
a radiant example of His Word made flesh.

Key Points

- The purpose of your getting unstuck and living an amazing life is bigger than you.

- God wants to show His immense power through you. He wants you to be His light to a world in darkness.

This morning, as I was preparing to speak at a women's retreat, this is what I heard in my spirit: "Speak to them about having big faith. If they are going to call themselves Christians, I need their faith to bring Me glory."

Perhaps you feel motivated to get unstuck and be unstoppable so you can finally live the life God imagined for you. But the purpose of your getting unstuck and living that amazing life is bigger than you. Just look around you. Consider what you see on television, in your community, in popular music, in the world at large. It is a mess. Values have eroded. Common courtesies have too often disappeared. What is considered the norm on television would have been appalling just 30 years ago. And people are hurting. They are searching for answers. They are looking for a miracle, for transformation. They are looking to role models who can show them the way to happiness and a better life. But sadly, if they look to the life of the average Christian today, I'm not so sure they see the kind of power that would intrigue them to try Jesus.

Getting unstuck is not just about your pushing past issues and challenges. It is about being a light in a dark world—living in such a way that your courage, love, and boldness shine brightly to those who cross your path. God wants to use you. He wants you to be His ambassador to the world around you so that He might show His immense power through you. He wants the unbeliever to be able to look at your life and say, "Wow, what's her secret weapon? Where does she find the strength? What motivates her? Where did she get such wisdom?" He wants the world to see His church as a source of answers, and He can't do that if the church is made up of a bunch of stuck people too scared to change.

So I challenge you right now to commit yourself to showing God's Word to be true in your life. If you believe that "with God all things are possible" (Matthew 19:26), then aren't you ready to be a radiant example of that?

> We are therefore Christ's ambassadors, as though God were
> making his appeal through us (2 Corinthians 5:20).

Get Moving!

In what way(s) is God prompting you to step out in faith and be a radiant example of His Word made flesh?

_____

_____

_____

_____

_____

_____

Prayer

Dear Lord, I want to be Your ambassador. I want Your power to work in me, to transform my life and give life to those around me. Show me where fear has kept me bound and empower me with the courage and boldness to have a breakthrough that glorifies Your name. Amen.

Conclusion

I'm nestled in a swinging daybed on the back deck of a wood cabin 90 miles north of Atlanta, gazing out at the North Georgia mountains. Bundled in my warmest jacket with a blanket snuggled around my feet, it is a cool 50 degrees today. I'm a beach girl at heart, having been born in Florida, but I spent the majority of my growing-up years near the mountains of Germany and Colorado. And something about getting away to the mountains seems to connect me to my heart's desires. Maybe it is the visual of being high above all else, having a perspective that empowers me to see peaks and valleys and multiple mountaintops. The quiet grandeur of the mountains seems to heighten my ability to hear His still, small voice—as though the vision of a grand, majestic mountain inspires me to see the vision God is whispering to my soul. Crisp, clean air and the occasional whistle of a hooting owl or chirping red cardinal awakens my heart's own music. This week, I came here to hear the song this book will sing. To get a vision of where God wants the journey to lead you and me.

In the midst of writing these words, I look up and to my delight, see an eagle flying—no, floating—above the bare treetops over the valley before me. Her wings are outstretched as she sails through the air. She is free and flying—just as I know God wants you to be. Every once in a while, she flaps her wings a few times and then floats again, effortlessly it seems.

You too can soar effortlessly, shaking off the fears and hindrances—both seen and unseen—that keep you from flying to new heights in every area of your life...your relationship, work, health, finances, and spiritual life. You can stop playing small and live the big, full, amazing life God has for you.

You see, despite the fact that this is my tenth book, I've been stuck many times. When I tell people I'm a recovering procrastinator, they seem not to believe me. That's because they only see the end result: a book in their hand. But from my perspective, I know the torturous path of hesitation, avoidance, procrastination, and beating myself up that reigned before I finally managed to get unstuck and get on a roll. Today, less than two months into my marriage, I am here in the mountains with my family. This time last year, I was single with no children. Today, I'm married with two bonus daughters. No longer in the center of the city, I live in what I call rural suburbia—a place I unexpectedly like. No traffic. I see farms and horses on my way to the interstate. And I can get to the city in under an hour if I want to.

When I finished these words, I looked up again. The eagle is soaring with her friends now. A sign perhaps, that it's time for us to soar. Let's journey together to the heights of where God is calling you. There is something more, something bigger, something better waiting for you. It's time to get unstuck so you can live the amazing life God is calling you to.

Career Clogger Quiz

Discover your primary career fear—the one that most threatens to trip you up. You dream of a more fulfilling career…but why aren't you going for it? Some of us insist, "I just don't have the time" or, "If I had more money, I'd do what I want." Peel back the layers, though, and you'll find the real reason for your hesitation: Fear.

But what exactly are you afraid of? Take this quiz and discover the real fear that's keeping you stuck. Circle the answer that would be your most prominent thought if faced with the stated scenario. Tally which letters you circled most in response to the questions. Then turn to the answer key to get insights that will help you muster the courage to conquer it. You can also take this quiz and four others for free online by clicking on the "Assessments" tab at www.valorieburton.com.

1. You've secretly wanted to do something new at work. A position finally opens up in the department in your company you'd really like to work in. It's a higher pressure job, but the rewards are big. You…

a) Think about applying for it, but wonder if you have a shot at it since some other candidates might have more experience.

b) Get anxious about the pressure. What if you can't keep up?

c) Wonder how you'll break the news to your boss. She thinks you're happy in her department.

d) Can't stop thinking about all the negative things that might happen if you "rock the boat" at this stage in your career.

e) Go for it. This is exactly the break you've been waiting for!

2. The business you launched on the side starts to really take off. You could finally quit your day job and do this full-time! This has been your goal for years. You...

a) Aren't so sure your part-time success will translate into full-time success.

b) Are afraid of being solely responsible for your own paycheck.

c) Hesitate to tell your friends because they'll think you're crazy to quit your day job.

d) Start asking, "What if I go broke? What if I'm out on the street and can't find another job?"

e) Check the calendar to see how soon you can quit and turn in your letter of resignation.

3. You were just laid off from the publishing house where you've been working for ten years. You've always daydreamed about becoming an interior designer, but there was never a good time to pursue that dream. You...

a) Know the odds of success in interior design are slim so you just look for another publishing gig.

b) Realize you love designing as a hobby, but cringe when you think of the expectations you'll have to meet when working with actual *paying* clients.

c) Worry about a negative reaction when you announce your decision to colleagues and family.

d) Don't want to start at the bottom in a new industry. It's safer to stick with what you know.

e) Are secretly happy you've been laid off. It was the push you needed to take that leap of faith.

4. You always wanted to be a schoolteacher. Discouraged by the starting salaries, you went into pharmaceutical sales instead. With a recent inheritance from your great-aunt and your spouse's new pay raise, you could live just fine on a smaller salary. You...

a) Remember the unruly kids in your neighborhood. Can you really manage a bunch of eight-year-olds?

b) Think, "At least with my sales job, I don't have the pressure of 25 kids relying on me every day."

c) Don't pursue it because you'll be seen as wishy-washy for making such a dramatic career change.

d) Wonder if you're being irresponsible. What if your spouse loses his job unexpectedly?

e) Start looking for teaching jobs right away. You can't believe your good fortune!

5. Your boss is impressed with your performance and recently asked you about your long-term career goals. The buzz around the office is that she's about to get a big promotion and you have a feeling she's going to recommend you for her job. You...

a) Are worried you don't know enough to succeed at that job yet. Failing could sabotage your career.

b) Are irritated that performing well means people are always trying to give you more responsibility.

c) Think, "What about Jeff and Marci? They have more seniority. This is going to cause quite a stir."

d) Become paralyzed with fear as you imagine every bad thing that could happen if you mess this up.

e) Are excited that you might get such a great opportunity. You work hard. You deserve it.

6. You declare to a friend that you are ready to make a career change, but you just don't know where to start. She offers to introduce you to a contact of hers who could open some doors. You...

   a) Never call the guy. It's a tough job market. It would be better to wait until the economy picks up.

   b) Feel a knot in your stomach. It's time to step up or shut up. Are you really ready for change?

   c) Think, "This man isn't going to take me seriously. I don't have enough experience."

   d) Back down from your declaration. The idea of changing careers is just too overwhelming.

   e) Thank her for her offer. You'll contact the person later today and invite him to lunch.

7. Since moving 1,000 miles away from your family to land your first "real" job, you've wanted to get back closer to home. Your hometown is a bigger city with lots to do. Lately you've been feeling more homesick than usual and it is negatively affecting how you feel about your job. You...

   a) Don't get your hopes up. Your chances of finding a job in your hometown are slim right now.

   b) Worry your skills might not be as prized in a big city where the competition is much stiffer.

   c) Imagine your friends and family will think you couldn't make it on your own.

   d) Think, "Who knows what will happen if I give up the career I've built here? Leaving is a big risk."

   e) Call everyone you know back home who could help you. Surely, there's a job with your name on it.

8. **Your parents saved and sacrificed to put you through college and law school. Now, you feel guilty that you don't like your work. It sounded like a great career choice, but you have no passion for it and actually dread getting up and going to your law firm every day. You...**

   a) Make yourself suck it up and work harder. You can do this. Your motto is, "Never ever give up."

   b) Do just enough to satisfy the higher-ups, but not enough to get saddled with a heavy caseload.

   c) Wouldn't dare tell your parents. They would be so disappointed in you.

   d) Wish you could pursue a new path, but you enjoy your lifestyle too much to take a pay cut.

   e) Know it will be upsetting to your family, but you take steps toward a career you are passionate about.

9. **You work for a growing startup company. Your boss gets fired and you'd love to have her job. You feel quite confident your ideas and energy would be a great asset to the company. Problem is, your résumé doesn't show enough years of experience to qualify for the position. You...**

   a) Don't waste your time applying. You are unlikely to get it anyway.

   b) Think you can do it, but have a few doubts. You ask yourself, "Am I really up for this challenge?"

   c) Pretend not to want the job. You don't want to appear presumptuous.

   d) Worry you'll suffer the fate of your boss—getting axed if the company isn't happy with you.

   e) Go to the hiring manager and make a case for why you're the best candidate for the job.

10. Your doctor suggests your string of recent health challenges is due to work-related stress and the long hours you spend at the office. She "prescribes" regular vacation and a more sane work schedule—both of which are possible. She even suggests it will make you more productive. You...

   a) Are afraid if you work less, your performance will suffer. So you don't change a thing.

   b) Think, "If I start being more productive in less time, they'll just give me more work."

   c) Ignore the doctor's orders. You won't be seen as a team player if you leave the office by 6 o'clock.

   d) Say, "I'll be stressed on vacation thinking about the pile of work waiting for me when I come back."

   e) Agree with your doctor. It's time to make some changes and give yourself a break.

11. You enjoy your job as an editor, but you also dream of being a novelist. It would give you so much satisfaction to finally write that book you've been thinking about for years—and get it published. Your best friend asks you over lunch why you don't get started now. You...

   a) Tell her it's too hard to get a publisher. Why write a book if no one's going to publish it?

   b) Are anxious about putting yourself out there like that—for your work to be scrutinized and critiqued.

   c) Are worried how your employer will feel about your promoting a book. You haven't even asked.

   d) Think, "What if the book really takes off? How will I handle my job, the publicity, the kids?"

   e) Say, "That's a great question. *Why don't I* get started now?" You start writing this week.

12. You've been unemployed and looking for a new job in the same field for four months now. You actually want to enter a new field of work, but haven't given yourself permission to try. You're not really sure where to start. You...

a) Decide to stick with what you know. Why risk failure?

b) Think, "What if I land a job in this new field and they figure out I don't really know what I'm doing?"

c) Would rather not face more rejection. It's been hard enough getting "no's" in one field, let alone two.

d) Think, "What if I don't like this new career after all? What if I regret making a change?"

e) Start pursuing jobs in this new field, too. Who knows? You might get exactly what you want.

13. Your significant other suggests you might be happier at work if you spent less time with the negative gossips you have lunch with every day. They seem to see the glass as half empty and it's affecting your attitude. You know your sweetheart is right. You...

a) Start beating yourself up for wasting so much time being negative. You know better.

b) Make excuses about why you're not happy and insist your negative coworkers are not to blame.

c) Fear the social repercussions at work of removing yourself from the clique.

d) Know he's right, but don't want to give up being "in the know."

e) Are tired of those energy-draining conversations and make new lunch plans starting tomorrow.

14. Your annual review is coming up next week and your boss has asked everyone to come to their review with one idea that would improve their productivity. You'd love the option of working from home two days a week, but no one else in the department currently gets that perk. You...

a) Are afraid to ask because you don't really trust yourself to get work done with the TV so close by.

b) Don't like the fact that all eyes will be on you if you are the first person to get this opportunity.

c) Worry your coworkers will be jealous or your boss will reject your request as selfish.

d) Are concerned that if you're not physically in the office, you will lose some influence.

e) Prepare to make your request during your review next week and hope she says *yes*.

15. You've worked in a bank for the last eight years, but you're tired of sitting behind a desk all day. After volunteering at a children's hospital the last few months, you're surprised to discover what you really want to do—become a nurse. It will take two years of classes to make it happen. You...

a) Were not the best student so you're not sure if going back to school is a good idea.

b) Will have to be engaged in your work every day—lives are at stake. Do you have the energy for that?

c) Do nothing. You dread dealing with family members who believe change is always bad and stability is always good.

d) Are afraid working and going to school at the same time will be too overwhelming.

e) Enroll in courses at a local college. Life's too short not to pursue your dreams!

Answer Key

Mostly "A" responses
Fear of Failure

You are so afraid of the possibility of failure that you'd rather not even try. You probably learned somewhere along the way to play it safe, but it's time to step out of your comfort zone. It may sound obvious, but think about it—when you leave your comfort zone, you will feel *un*comfortable. I have found that clients who fear failure often take it very personally. They say, "I'm a failure" rather than "I failed" or "That didn't go so well." Many are perfectionists or procrastinators who want a guarantee of the outcome before they take steps onto a new path.

Sound familiar? Give yourself permission to be imperfect. Take baby steps by setting small goals to build your confidence. When the question "What if I fail?" evokes paralyzing fear, answer it. Imagine you've made the decision to pursue the career of your dreams and it doesn't work out. What if that happened? What would you do? By answering your own "what if?" questions, you ease your fear and create a Plan B that can give you the mental clarity and courage to conquer your fear of failure.

Mostly "B" responses
Fear of Success

You're fairly confident in your abilities, but don't like the pressure of maintaining success once you have it. Success means more responsibility and higher expectations. You may even wonder if you can keep it up. You may feel it's easier to be the big fish in a little pond than to venture into bigger waters. Don't sell yourself short. You are capable of more than you think you are. But you'll never know until you allow yourself to be stretched and challenged. When you do, you'll earn a new level of confidence and experience what it means to really live.

Another fear some of my clients in this category experience is one that researchers call the "Imposter Syndrome." And women suffer from it more than men—the feeling that people will find out you're really not as great as they think you are. If this is you, beware of how you explain your successes. Rather than brushing your success off to luck or circumstances, give yourself credit for your talent, tenacity, and other personal attributes that will lead to success on your new path.

Mostly "C" responses
Fear of Disapproval

Because you often seek the approval of others before making a change, you get stuck when you don't get that approval or perceive you won't get it. You may also seek validation in things, titles, and money. To move toward the life you really want, you'll need to push past this unhealthy "approval addiction." Make a choice to value your own approval more than others' and your authentic self will find the right path.

Sometimes this issue manifests as a fear of rejection. You take *no* personally. Because your dreams require you to ask others for help, you find yourself stuck. Some who fear disapproval also fear they're "not good enough." This translates into statements such as, "I'm not young enough/attractive enough/thin enough/smart enough." Rather than focusing on what you see as weaknesses, focus on your strengths. What are your strengths? Make a list. Your right path will tap into your signature strengths—those innate gifts and abilities that you own, enjoy, and frequently use.

Mostly "D" responses
Fear of Losing Control

You're afraid that if you follow your heart, you'll lose everything—financially, professionally, or even in your relationships. You feel overwhelmed by the prospect of change. For many of my clients, the key to overcoming this fear is putting their fears in perspective. Is it time for you to do the same?

Some whose primary fear is losing control can be categorized as a "catastrophizer," a psychology term that describes what happens when our thoughts spiral out of control as we imagine the worst-case irrational outcomes for the future. For example, you dream of pursuing your new career, but within seconds imagine yourself living on the streets after you fail miserably.

If this describes your thinking pattern, University of Pennsylvania resilience researcher Dr. Karen Reivich suggests interrupting your negative thought spiral by first imagining an equally irrational best-case scenario. For example, you become so amazing at your new job that you get promoted five times in the first year, triple your salary, and are profiled in the national media as the poster child for your field. Once you jolt yourself out of your negative spiral by creating a positive spiral, ask yourself, "What's the most likely scenario?" You likely will not triple your salary or end up on the streets, but you will transition responsibly one step at a time.

Mostly "E" responses
Unstuck and Unstoppable

Congratulations! You understand an important truth: *Everyone* feels fear. And you know a key to success is not letting it control you. When you feel fear, you don't let it stop you. With practice, you've developed the courage you need to move forward despite your fears. Your courage and confidence empower you to find the right path for you and stay the course when you encounter bumps on the road.

Justo Gonzalez

About the Author

A bestselling author and Certified Personal and Executive Coach who has served clients in over 40 states and eight countries, Valorie Burton has written nine books on personal development, including *Successful Women Think Differently* and *Happy Women Live Better*. She is the founder of The CaPP Institute, providing tools and training that build resilience, well-being, and productivity for life and work.

She has been a regular contributor on CNN, HLN, and the *Today* show, where she gives practical career and life advice. She has also been featured in and on *The Dr. Oz Show*, NPR, Oprah Radio, *Ebony, Essence, "O" The Oprah Magazine,* the *Chicago Tribune, LA Times,* and hundreds of others. Valorie's corporate clientele includes multimillion-dollar businesses such as Accenture, Black Entertainment Television (BET), Deloitte, General Mills, McDonald's Corp., and many more.

Join 25,000 subscribers to her weekly e-newsletter at www.valorieburton.com and visit her company site at www.cappinstitute.com.